English for Secretaries   Teacher's book

English for Secretaries

Teacher's Book

Oxford University Press 1978

Oxford University Press
Walton Street, Oxford OX2 6DP

Oxford London Glasgow New York
Toronto Melbourne Wellington
Cape Town Ibadan Nairobi
Dar Es Salaam Lusaka Kuala Lumpur
Singapore Jakarta Hong Kong Tokyo
Delhi Bombay Calcutta Madras
Karachi

ISBN 0 19 457195 5 (student's book)
ISBN 0 19 457196 3 (teacher's book)
ISBN 0 19 457197 1 (tape set)
ISBN 0 19 457198 x (cassette set)

© Oxford University Press 1977

English for Secretaries was researched, developed and written by the Oxford University Press English Language Teaching Development Unit.
The course was originally developed for Atlas Copco AB and Telefonaktiebolaget LM Ericsson, Stockholm, Sweden.

This book is sold subject to the condition that it shall not, by way of trade or otherwise, be lent, re-sold, hired out, or otherwise circulated without the publisher's prior consent in any form of binding or cover other than that in which it is published and without a similar condition including this condition being imposed on the subsequent purchaser.

All rights reserved. No part of this publication may be reproduced, stored in a retrieval system, or transmitted, in any form or by any means, electronic, mechanical, photocopying, recording or otherwise, without the prior permission of Oxford University Press.

Printed in Great Britain by
G. A. Pindar & Son Ltd., Scarborough

Contents

Introductory notes	Material	1
	Structure and aims of the course	1
	Use of the material	5
Unit 1	Unit Summary	11
	Introductory Recording: Tapescript and Comprehension Questions	12
	Text: Comprehension Questions	14
	Key to the Exercises	16
	Language Laboratory Part 1: Tapescript	17
	Language Laboratory Part 2: Tapescript	21
	Role Simulation	25
	Key to 'What is this?'	26
Unit 2	Unit Summary	27
	Introductory Recording: Tapescript and Comprehension Questions	28
	Text: Comprehension Questions	31
	Key to the Exercises	32
	Language Laboratory Part 1: Tapescript	33
	Language Laboratory Part 2: Tapescript	37
	Role Simulation	40
	Key to 'What is this?'	42
Unit 3	Unit Summary	43
	Introductory Recording: Tapescript and Comprehension Questions	45
	Text: Comprehension Questions	47
	Key to the Exercises	48
	Language Laboratory Part 1: Tapescript	49
	Language Laboratory Part 2: Tapescript	53
	Role Simulation	56
	Key to 'What is this?'	56
Unit 4	Unit Summary	57
	Introductory Recording: Tapescript and Comprehension Questions	58
	Text: Comprehension Questions	61
	Key to the Exercises	62
	Language Laboratory Part 1: Tapescript	63
	Language Laboratory Part 2: Tapescript	67
	Role Simulation	71
	Key to 'What is this?'	73

Unit 5	Unit Summary	74
	Introductory Recording: Tapescript and Comprehension Questions	75
	Text: Comprehension Questions	77
	Key to the Exercises	79
	Language Laboratory Part 1: Tapescript	79
	Language Laboratory Part 2: Tapescript	83
	Role Simulation	87
	Key to 'What is this?'	89
Unit 6	Unit Summary	90
	Introductory Recording: Tapescript and Comprehension Questions	91
	Text: Comprehension Questions	94
	Key to the Exercises	95
	Language Laboratory Part 1: Tapescript	97
	Language Laboratory Part 2: Tapescript	100
	Role Simulation	103
	Key to 'What is this?'	104
Unit 7	Unit Summary	105
	Introductory Recording: Tapescript and Comprehension Questions	106
	Text: Comprehension Questions	109
	Key to the Exercises	110
	Language Laboratory Part 1: Tapescript	111
	Language Laboratory Part 2: Tapescript	115
	Role Simulation	118
	Key to 'What is this?'	119
Unit 8	Unit Summary	120
	Introductory Recording: Tapescript and Comprehension Questions	121
	Text: Comprehension Questions	124
	Key to the Exercises	125
	Language Laboratory Part 1: Tapescript	127
	Language Laboratory Part 2: Tapescript	130
	Role Simulation	133
	Key to 'What is this?'	134
Unit 9	Unit Summary	135
	Introductory Recording: Tapescript and Comprehension Questions	136
	Text: Comprehension Questions	139

	Key to the Exercises	140
	Language Laboratory Part 1: Tapescript	141
	Language Laboratory Part 2: Tapescript	145
	Role Simulation	148
	Key to 'What is this?'	149
Unit 10	Unit Summary	150
	Introductory Recording: Tapescript and Comprehension Questions	151
	Text: Comprehension Questions	153
	Key to the Exercises	154
	Language Laboratory Part 1: Tapescript	156
	Language Laboratory Part 2: Tapescript	159
	Role Simulation	162
	Key to 'What is this?'	162
Unit 11	Unit Summary	163
	Introductory Recording: Tapescript and Comprehension Questions	164
	Text: Comprehension Questions	167
	Key to the Exercises	168
	Language Laboratory Part 1: Tapescript	169
	Language Laboratory Part 2: Tapescript	173
	Role Simulation	176
	Key to 'What is this?'	177
Unit 12	Unit Summary	178
	Introductory Recording: Tapescript and Comprehension Questions	179
	Text: Comprehension Questions	181
	Key to the Exercises	183
	Language Laboratory Part 1: Tapescript	184
	Language Laboratory Part 2: Tapescript	189
	Role Simulation	191
	Key to 'What is this?'	192

Introductory notes

Aim of the course The course is designed to improve the secretary's ability to function efficiently and confidently in English in her job. Emphasis is therefore placed on developing those language skills that are most frequently required of a secretary, within the situations in which she commonly finds herself in her office.

Length of the course The course provides material for a minimum of 72 lessons of 45 minutes (54 clock hours) in the classroom and language laboratory, and a further 12 clock hours' homework.

Level of entry The course is intended for secretaries who are at an intermediate level of attainment. It presupposes that the student has already covered, but not thoroughly mastered, the common grammatical structures of English.

Size of classes The course is best suited to classes of not more than ten students.

Material

The course consists of:

A **Student's Book** containing all the student's material and a glossary.

A **Teacher's Book** containing Unit Summaries, Comprehension Questions, Keys to the Exercises, Tapescripts and Roles.

A set of six twin-track **Language Laboratory Tapes** or **Cassettes**.

Structure and aims of the course

The course consists of twelve units. Each unit comprises:

Introductory Recording The purpose of the Introductory Recording is to present a common office situation with which the students can identify—eg taking a message for the boss, or talking to a visitor. These recordings are episodes in the working lives of secretaries in Schweibur, an imaginary Swiss company manufacturing office equipment. Each recording is linked to the Text that follows and thus acts as a stimulating entry point into the work of the unit.

Text The purpose of the Text is to introduce in an appropriate context the vocabulary and grammatical structures to be dealt with in the unit. Each Text is in a form relevant to the work of a secretary, such as a letter, a memo, etc.

Vocabulary Exercise(s) The purpose of the Vocabulary Exercise(s) is to increase the student's active command of relevant vocabulary, and to provide practice in distinguishing between shades of meaning and usage of apparently similar words.

Remedial Grammar Exercises and Drills It is assumed throughout the course that students will already have covered the basic grammatical structures of English, either through previous participation in a training programme, or at school.

As it is unlikely, however, that students will have thoroughly mastered these structures, each unit contains two or three grammatical structures for remedial treatment. The structures dealt with are those known to cause difficulty to learners. The tools provided for the teacher to handle these structures are firstly Exercises designed primarily for oral, classroom use, and secondly Language Laboratory Drills.

Pronunciation Practice The secretary is frequently the first person in any organization whom members of the public have any contact with, whether they are telephoning or visiting. It is important, therefore, that the secretary's pronunciation of English should be clear, and preferably without any marked accent.

The course provides ear-training and practice in vowel sounds that learners frequently confuse, in the rhythm of English, and in those intonation patterns which are most likely to be required by the secretary in the course of her duties.

Dialogue The purpose of the Dialogue is to provide practice in pronunciation and in intonation, and also to improve the secretary's ability to handle common, clearly defined situations with which she is likely to be confronted during the course of her work. In the second half of the course the secretary is given the opportunity to substitute alternative expressions.

Correspondence The ability to handle correspondence in English is of great importance to to the secretary in her daily work. A task she often has to undertake is the correction of drafts and letters written in English by her boss, or by other members of her department.

Each unit therefore contains a draft letter containing typical mistakes in English, to be corrected in class under the guidance of the teacher.

The grammatical mistakes written into these draft letters are confined to points that have already been covered in the course.

The purpose of this section of each unit is to provide the student with the opportunity to develop her skill in spotting and correcting mistakes made in correspondence, and also to act as revision and reinforcement of the structures and vocabulary already studied.

Telegrams The purpose of this section is to provide practice in decoding and encoding telegrams.

'Gambit' Drills The term 'Gambit' in this course is used to refer to formulae or expressions that a secretary whose mother tongue is English uses in certain clearly defined situations. She uses these formulae to achieve a particular object or to carry out a particular function, frequently on behalf of her boss.

For example, a secretary frequently has to relay messages from her boss to others. A suitable expression to use when performing this function would be:

I'm afraid Mr Gräber is in a meeting at the moment, **Mr** Smith. **Would Friday at twelve be convenient**?

As the ability to use these 'gambits' in their appropriate context is important for the efficient secretary, each unit contains two 'Gambit' Drills.

Active Listening Each unit contains passages for Active Listening. The number and form of the passages varies from unit to unit, and a brief summary of the passages is given in each Unit Summary.

The purpose of the passages for Active Listening is to improve the student's ability to understand telephone messages, recorded instructions from the boss, dictated letters, etc, so that she can take the required action.

At the beginning of the course, comprehension questions are provided in the Student's Book. These comprehension questions should be regarded as prompts to the student, in that they draw the student's attention to the salient points of the passage she is listening to. The number of these questions is progressively reduced until the only instruction to the students is, for example, *Write down the message*. At the beginning of the course the student is encouraged to listen to the passage more than once before answering the questions, but as the course progresses, the student is told not to rewind the tape. During the course, telephone distortion is added to the recordings. On completion of the course the secretary will have had extensive practice in taking telephone messages and recorded instructions in a lifelike situation.

Role Simulation One of the secretary's most important functions is to meet her boss's visitors. If her boss is in any way delayed, she is expected to look after the visitors until he comes, and this naturally involves conversation. Furthermore, visitors frequently come to a secretary for information, etc. This may range from a request for paper clips to advice on where to buy presents.

In order to provide practice in handling visitors, each unit contains a Role Simulation. This revolves round a central situational theme. For example, the students may be asked to imagine that they have to help a visitor deal with a problem, or that they have to relay information from their boss. The teacher's material contains ten variations on each theme in the form of 'roles' which provide the necessary background information and set guidelines for the ensuing conversation. Sometimes these roles are intended for distribution to the students to help them play their role of secretary. In other units, the roles are intended only for the use of the teacher, who is required to play the part of the visitor. In such cases, the student is given no help in the acting out of her role other than a general explanation by the teacher of the situational theme.

The Role Simulation thus provides practice in handling visitors in certain common situations. It also provides a realistic framework within which the student can activate the vocabulary, gambits and structures she has already practised in more controlled situations in the classroom and language laboratory.

Homework

Each unit contains a letter to be written for homework. The purpose of this component of the course is to introduce the students to certain common formulae frequently found in correspondence, such as:

Would you please confirm that . . .

and to give them practice in their use.

The formulae are grouped together under such headings as 'Expressing dissatisfaction and complaining' or 'Asking for approval'. To practice these formulae, the students are given a letter to which they must reply. They are also given a draft outline for this reply which controls the overall framework of their letter but allows them to select appropriate phrases from their repertoire of formulae. The number of formulae introduced per unit is reduced as the course progresses, whilst the replying letter gradually becomes more complex.

Use of the material

Where timetabling permits, the materials are best handled as shown in the following diagram. In the diagram each block represents a lesson of forty-five minutes' duration.

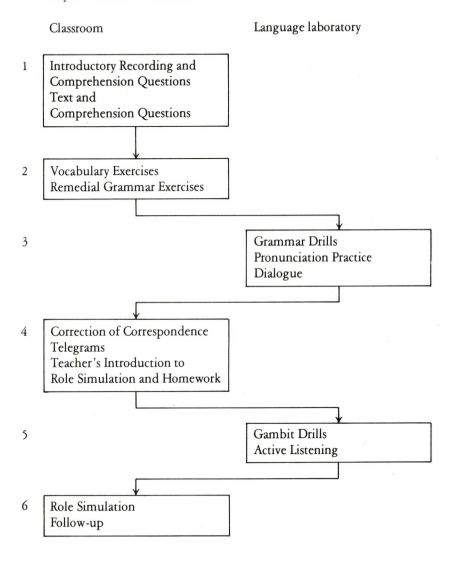

Thus each unit contains material for a minimum of four and a half hours' work—three hours in the classroom and one and a half hours in the language laboratory. In addition, there is material for one hour of homework per unit, bringing the total up to five and a half hours' work per unit.

Naturally, this can only be a rough guide. It is left to the teacher to calculate the amount of time required for each part of a unit according to the needs of the particular class. It is recognized that adjustment of this order of presentation may well be necessary to suit local conditions.

Unit Summary At the beginning of each unit there is a Unit Summary. This lists the contents of the unit and also contains any additional teaching notes required.

Introductory Recording The recording should be played through to the students without stopping. Comprehension questions are provided in the Teacher's Book so that the teacher can check the students' general understanding of the passage. These questions only aim to ascertain whether the students have followed the broad outline of the story and the attitudes of the characters. The Introductory Recording should be regarded as stimulus material which sets the scene and provides interest value for the rest of the unit. It is not intended for intensive study. The illustrations which open many of the units in the Student's Book depict the situations in these recordings.

The material for this component of the course consists of:
Recording	(Unit Tape)
Tapescript	(Teacher's Book)
Comprehension questions	(Teacher's Book)
Illustration	(Student's Book)

Text The teacher should begin by linking the Introductory Recording to the Text as outlined in the Unit Summary. The teacher may ask the students to prepare the Text in advance of the lesson, or deal with it in class. Whichever method is adopted, the teacher must make sure that the new vocabulary is understood by the students. For the convenience of the teacher, a number of comprehension questions on the Text are provided in the Teacher's Book.

The material for this component of the course consists of:
Text	(Student's Book)
Comprehension questions and suggested answers	(Teacher's Book)

Vocabulary Exercise(s) The teacher should use these exercises not only to check comprehension of the meaning and usage of the key words, but also to explain other vocabulary used in these Exercises. The Vocabulary Exercises are best handled orally in the class, after completion of the Text.

The material for this component of the course consists of:
One or more exercises   (Student's Book)
Key to the exercises   (Teacher's Book)

Remedial Grammar Exercises and Drills

Each Unit Summary lists the grammatical points to be studied in that unit.

The Exercises can be done orally in class as supporting material for the teacher's own introduction to the structures, or as homework for revision purposes. The Language Laboratory Drills should be seen as an integral part of the establishment of the structure within the student's working knowledge of English, and they should therefore be used as a reinforcement of the teacher's work in the classroom. A possible approach to each grammatical item would be:

First Step:	Oral introduction by the teacher, leading from selected sentences in the Text or the Introductory Recording
Second Step:	The relevant exercise done orally in class (or as homework)
Third Step:	Intensive oral practice in the language laboratory
Fourth Step:	The transfer of this knowledge in a less tightly controlled situation, as provided by the Role Simulation.

It is left to the teacher to decide on the amount of oral introduction necessary for a particular structure, according to the relative strengths or weaknesses of the class.

The material for this component of the course consists of:
Two or three exercises   (Student's Book)
Key to the exercises   (Teacher's Book)
Language Laboratory
Drills 1 and 2   (Unit Tape)
Tapescript   (Teacher's Book)
Examples and notes for
the student   (Student's Book)

Pronunciation Practice

The Unit Summary lists the vowel sounds or intonation patterns to be practised in that unit.

Full instructions to the student are provided on the Unit Tape. In this component of the course, limericks are used as a device for practising the rhythm and vowel sounds of English. Since some of these limericks contain vocabulary that the student may not be familiar with, teachers would be advised to go over them very briefly at the beginning of the language laboratory period or in a preceding class.

The material for this component of the course consists of:
Recorded exercises   (Unit Tape)
Tapescript   (Teacher's Book)
Notes for the student   (Student's Book)

Dialogue	The Unit Summary shows the theme of the Dialogue for that unit.
	In Units 1 to 3 the student is asked to: Listen to the Dialogue. Repeat key words and phrases leading to complete utterances (backchaining). Speak at the same time as the secretary (shadowing). Take the part of the secretary.
	In Units 4 and 5, shadowing is omitted.
	In Units 6 to 12 the student is asked to: Listen to the Dialogue. Repeat key words and phrases leading to complete utterances (backchaining). Take the part of the secretary. Practise using the alternative expressions, with her book open. Practise using the alternative expressions, with her book closed.
	The material for this component of the course consists of: Recorded dialogue (Unit Tape) Tapescript (Teacher's Book) The secretary's role in the Dialogue + alternative expressions (Student's Book)
Correspondence	This is best done orally in the classroom, thereby giving the teacher the opportunity to clarify mistakes immediately. Since there is more than one correct way of expressing the ideas contained in the letters, the teacher can use this opportunity to discuss alternative correct versions.
	The material for this component of the course consists of: Draft letter (Student's Book) Suggested correct version (Teacher's Book)
Telegrams	These are best handled orally in the classroom.
	The material for this component of the course consists of: Telegrams (Student's Book) Suggested solutions (Teacher's Book)
Gambit Drills	The Unit Summary lists the gambits to be practiced in that unit.
	The material for this component of the course consists of: Drills 3 and 4 (Unit Tape) Tapescript (Teacher's Book) Examples and notes for the student (Student's Book)

Active Listening	The Unit Summary lists the tasks required of the student in that Unit.

The material for this component of the course consists of:
Recorded passages   (Unit Tape)
Tapescript   (Teacher's Book)
Questions   (Student's Book and Teacher's Book)
Key to the correct answers   (Teacher's Book)

Role Simulation

The following procedure is suggested for handling the Role Simulation:

Before the Role Simulation session

First Step: Draw the students' attention to the explanation of the purpose of this component of the course as given in the Student's Book.

Second Step: Describe the situational framework for the Role Simulation as outlined in the Teacher's Book.

Third Step: In those units where roles are provided for the students the roles should be given out to the students in advance. (The roles may be copied from the Teacher's Book onto cards, for distribution.) Students should also be told of any other preparation needed for carrying out their roles.

Fourth Step: The teacher should prepare his role of visitor.

During the Role Simulation session

Fifth Step: The students and teacher should now act out their roles. The classroom should be made to look as much like an office as possible, and 'props' such as dummy telephones should be provided, if possible, in certain units.

Sixth Step: As the teacher himself is required to play a prominent part in the Role Simulation, the proceedings should be tape-recorded. The recording can be played back later and the mistakes discussed. On no account should the teacher correct the students during the Role Simulation.

The material for this component of the course consists of:
Teacher's notes and Roles   (Teacher's Book)
Explanation for the students   (Student's Book)

Homework

The Homework may be set at any appropriate point as the class works through the unit. Some class time should be set aside for checking that students understand the meanings of the formulae listed.

The material for this component of the course consists of:
Notes for the student   (Student's Book)

Glossary

The purpose of the Glossary is to help the student understand words which have been used in the course and which are likely to be outside her basic vocabulary. The *Englischer Mindestwortschatz* by Michael West and Hans G Hoffman, published by Hueber and Longman, has been taken as the basic vocabulary list, and only those words in the course which are not included in this list have been defined. Definitions are restricted to the meanings occurring in the course: eg **column** is defined only in the sense of **newspaper column**. The Glossary is an aid to the student, but it is not a dictionary. It should be supplemented where necessary by the use of a good dictionary such as the *Oxford Advanced Learner's Dictionary of Current English* by A S Hornby (Oxford University Press).

Unit 1

Unit Summary

Introductory Recording	In this first episode entitled 'The Fiftieth Anniversary', Mary Malone, a secretary with Schweibur, is welcoming a group of visitors to the company and answering their questions.
Text	The Text is an extract from a brochure on the company's activities which the visitors have been invited to take.
Vocabulary	Exercise A is a three-part exercise on vocabulary which appears in the Text.
Structures	1 Present simple/Present continuous (Exercise B and Drill 1). *We keep* paper clips in the cupboard. *We're expanding* our production facilities. 2 *It is/there is* (Exercise C). *It is* obvious that documents must be accessible. *There are* several ways of filing documents. 3 Comparison of adjectives (Exercise D and Drill 2). *convenient/more convenient.*
Pronunciation Practice	This deals with the difference between the vowel sounds [i] as in *beat* and [ɪ] as in *bit*. There is an ear-training exercise followed by repetition of a limerick.
Dialogue	The situation is that of booking rooms at a hotel.
Correspondence	There is a draft letter for correction.
Telegrams	There are four telegrams, two to be decoded and two to be encoded.
Gambits	Drill 3: Dealing with telephone calls in the absence of the boss. *I'm afraid Mr Gräber is . . . , Mr . . . . Can I . . . ?* Drill 4: Politely delaying a visitor. *Mr Gräber is expecting you. He's just . . . . If you'd care to take a seat, he'll be . . . .*
Active Listening	There are two passages in this unit. 1 A dictated letter. The student is not required to take down the whole

dictation, but has to answer questions of the type: *What were the last two words you heard?*

2   A telephone message. There are comprehension questions leading to the writing down of the message.

Role Simulation   The students are asked to imagine that they have been detailed to act as guides for a group of visitors to their company. They have to welcome the visitors, introduce themselves, offer to answer the visitors' questions and respond to the visitors' comments.

Homework   The written gambits introduced in this unit deal with:

Reference
Expressing wishes
Requests

Additional Notes

Exercise D   This is an oral exercise practising the comparative forms, designed to lead from simple responses to more open-ended discussion.

Step 1: The students should read the notes on the different hotels.

Step 2: Ask one student to say which hotel she would recommend for Mr Gräber and give a reason for it, eg:

I would recommend the Excelsior. It's very clean.

Ask the student why she chose the Excelsior rather than the George. Make sure that she answers using a comparative, eg:

Because it's cleaner.

Repeat this with each student, using different hotels. Only revise the forms of the comparative if this is necessary.

Step 3: Now ask a student to recommend a hotel. Instead of asking her why, as in Step 2, get a second student to disagree, using either Table A or Table B.

Step 4: Get the class to decide as a group which hotel to put Mr Gräber in.

Introductory Recording

Tapescript   In this course you will meet Mary Malone, personal secretary. She will carry out many of the normal jobs of a good secretary. She will show you how to do these effectively in English. Mary Malone works in Zurich, in Switzerland, for a company which produces office equipment. Its name is Schweibur.

The Fiftieth Anniversary

Schweibur, the well-known makers of office equipment, are fifty years old this month. Visitors are arriving in Zurich from branches and associated companies all over the world. They are gathering in the reception hall. Everyone has written his name on a label and pinned the label to his coat, for identification. Mary Malone, personal secretary to Mr Gräber, is acting as a guide. She is talking to a small group of visitors.

Malone: Good morning, and welcome to Zurich and welcome to Schweibur Head Office. We're very happy to have you with us on our fiftieth anniversary and we hope you are enjoying your visit to Switzerland and to us. I'd like to introduce myself to you all. I'm Mary Malone. I'm personal secretary to Mr Erich Gräber, who is the Assistant Manager of the Marketing Division—perhaps some of you have met him . . .

Chorus: (Mixed assent and dissent.)

Malone: Now . . . Mr Basri, how do you do? You've come a long way—from Djarkarta, I suppose.

Basri: Oh yes. Good morning.

Malone: Miss Chapman—Vancouver—that's even further, isn't it?

Chapman: Hi. How are you?

Malone: Mr Achebe. It's nice to have someone from our Lagos office.

Achebe: How do you do, Miss Malone. Thank you.

Malone: Mr Jensen—we've met before, of course. How's Copenhagen?

Jensen: Yes, Mary, we have. Copenhagen? It's better than ever.

Malone: Fine. Mr Takashi, welcome to Zurich.

Takashi: Ah, thank you.

Malone: And Mrs Sanchez—from Venezuela, I see.
Very pleased to see you. Now, if I can have your attention, a few words about our company. It is, of course, fifty years since Schweibur was started by Helmut Schranz, who died in 1957. At first there was just a small factory here in Zurich, and fewer than fifty employees. The company made mostly office furniture in wood and metal, for sale in Switzerland. In the 1930s there was a greater demand for . . . *(Fade)*

Malone: . . . and now we make every type of office equipment, from paper clips to closed circuit television. Now, from this reception point, we shall be going to one of our seminar rooms to watch a film about the company and its associates around the world—in Copenhagen, Dublin my home city, Vancouver, Caracus, Lagos and Djarkarta. Just before we go . . . are there any questions you'd like to ask?

Takashi: I have a question. About turnover. What is the turnover of Schweibur last year, please?

Malone: About a hundred and fifty million Swiss francs, Mr Takashi. 20 per cent more than the year before. Yes, Mrs Sanchez?

Sanchez: Look, I'm sorry, I have a problem. It's about my journey home. I think maybe I've been booked on the wrong flight. Is there someone who can help me, please? I'm so worried about this . . .

Malone: Yes, of course, Mrs Sanchez. Our travel department . . . (*Fade*)

Malone: . . . and you can all take a brochure about Schweibur from that table over there. Now—any more questions? Fine. Follow me, please.

Comprehension Questions

1. What sort of business does Schweibur do?
   They produce office equipment.

2. Where is their Head Office?
   In Zurich.

3. Which Department does Mary Malone work in?
   In the Marketing Division.

4. What is Mary Malone doing in the recording?
   She's talking to a group of visitors.

5. Why are all these visitors there?
   Schweibur is celebrating its fiftieth anniversary.

6. Are the visitors Swiss?
   No.

7. Can you remember any of their nationalities?
   Indonesian; Canadian; Nigerian; Danish; Japanese; Venezuelan.

8. What sort of company is Schweibur?
   It is a large international company.

9. What are the visitors going to do after Mary Malone has told them about the company?
   They're going to see a film about the company and its associates.

10. Two of the visitors asked Mary questions. Can you remember what they were about?
    One asked about the annual turnover and the other asked about booking tickets for the return flight.

Text: The Fiftieth Anniversary

Comprehension Questions

The words and phrases in italics are quoted verbatim from the text.

1. Why does the writer find it difficult to give an adequate picture of his company?
   Because he is writing *a small brochure*.

Introductory Recording

2   What can he do in the pages that follow?
    He *can only suggest what* his company does, *where* it does it and *how* it does it.

3   How many companies are there in the Schweibur group?
    The *Group comprises more than forty companies.*

4   Does the number of employees stay the same?
    No, *the staff are being constantly increased.* **or:** No, it doesn't.

5   Why (not)?
    Because of the *continuous expansion of the Group's activities.*

6   What kind of reputation do Schweibur have?
    They *have a (deserved) reputation for superb design and quality.*

7   How do they feel about this?
    They *are particularly proud* of it.

8   What has it given them?
    It has given them *a leading position in their field.*

9   Where are their Headquarters?
    They *are located on the outskirts of Zurich.*

10 How many people work there?
    About / *Some six thousand employees work* there.

11 Is their Zurich office their only office in Switzerland?
    No, they have other *Swiss subsidiaries.*

12 What production policy does the company pursue?
    They pursue a policy of *decentralization.*

13 Where are the Group plants?
    They *are situated throughout Switzerland.*

14 Where are they beginning to build new plants?
    They are *starting to build new plants in Lausanne and outside Geneva.*

15 How much do they intend to put into these plants and other facilities?
    They are *planning to invest seventy million dollars.*

16 When are they spending this money?
    They are spending it *over the next two years.*

17 What function does Group management have?
    It establishes *decisions and policies.*

18 Are these decisions and policies carried out only in Zurich?
    No, they *affect* operations in the *subsidiaries in Switzerland and other countries throughout the world.*

19 When was the employees' new restaurant opened?
    It was *inaugurated in 1975.*

20 Is it large enough?
    No, it isn't. **or:** No, they *are already expanding* it.

21 How do you know that?
    Because they *are already expanding* it.

22 How is the medical centre staffed?
    It *is staffed by two full-time doctors*.

Key to the Exercises

Exercise A

1 Our manufacturing company is *located* about ten minutes by taxi from here.

2 We intend to *expand* the employees' restaurant in the near future.

3 The typists' pool is *staffed* by nine full-time office juniors.

4 The Group is planning a *substantial* expansion of its production facilities.

5 Our Group *comprises* 33 subsidiaries in Europe alone.

6 We have a *leading* position in our field.

7 The general opinion of Schweibur is good. In fact, they have a very high *reputation*.

8 The quality of their products has *secured* them a leading position among manufacturers of office equipment.

9 Our *policy* is one of decentralization.

10 Schweibur are *currently* planning a new factory in Lausanne.

11 Decisions taken at Headquarters *affect* the company's operations throughout the world.

12 The exhibition hall was *inaugurated in 1976*.

Exercise B

Mary Malone: . . . Now, the filing cabinets are over here. I *always keep* files that Mr Gräber is likely to want here in the office. He *likes* to have the files he *is currently working* on in his own office and of course dead files we *store* in the department's central filing system.

Miss Schneider: Yes, I *see*. I *suppose* there's an index, is there?

Mary Malone: Yes, I *am retyping* it at the moment. Here we are. It *probably looks* rather confusing, but I *expect* you'll soon get the hang of it. We *use* a numerical system, which I'm sure you *know* all about. Each subsidiary *has* an initial code number: 3 for example *refers* to our factory in Clermont-Ferrand, and the other numbers *refer* to particular subject areas. Mr Gräber *is thinking* of reorganizing it, but I *hope* he *doesn't* as I *find* it's efficient enough as it is.

Key to the Exercises

Miss Schneider: I *see*. Where *do you keep* things like staples and paper clips?

Mary Malone: Over in the cupboard. It's a bit on the full side, and I *am trying* to get a proper cupboard for storage from Office Services, but they *are not being* very helpful at the moment.

Miss Schneider: Am I responsible for ordering the things I need? I mean, *do I indent* for odds and ends from Office Services or *do I order* them myself?

Mary Malone: You *have to* indent for them, although it's inconvenient, and then they *take* a day or so to send them up, which is why I *like* to order in plenty of time. Now, can I show you this circulation list? Mr Gräber *has to* write a quarterly report, statistics of sales and so on, which you . . .

Exercise C

1. There are a number of advantages in using an alphabetical system.
2. There are rules for putting files in alphabetical order.
3. It is advisable for each department to adopt its own system.
4. It is clear that the geographical system is best for the export department.
5. It is difficult to use a numerical system without an index.
6. There isn't enough room to keep all the correspondence in the department.
7. It is usual to transfer old letters to dead files.
8. There is a good reason for keeping photographs in horizontal files.
9. There are also advantages in having a vertical storage cabinet.
10. It is annoying to find a file missing.

Exercise D

As this is an open-ended exercise, no key can be provided.

Language Laboratory Part 1: Tapescript

Drill 1

Miss Malone is secretary to the Assistant Marketing Manager of Schweibur. She is talking to a visitor.

1. (Example) Your production is extremely varied, isn't it?
   Yes, we produce a wide variety of equipment.

2. (Example) Is it true there's a large expansion programme?
   Yes, we're expanding to meet increased demand for our products.

3. The company must provide employment for quite a lot of people then?
   Yes, we employ well over two thousand in Zurich alone.

4. I see the builders are pulling down some walls in here. Is there to be some sort of extension?
   Yes, we're extending the offices to give us more space.

5. I suppose that means quite a bit of reorganization for you.
   Yes, we're reorganizing the whole filing system in the Marketing Division.

6 That must cause some storage problems.
Yes, we're storing all our files in these cupboards till the new office is ready.

7 Are these files often used for reference?
Yes, we refer to them whenever there's any enquiry about staff.

8 Are you responsible for the compilation of statistics?
Yes, we compile statistics for the quarterly reports.

Drill 2

Miss Schmidt is a secretary in the Travel Department. She is often asked to recommend a hotel to visiting agents or customers. Listen to how she does this.

1 (Example) I don't want anything too expensive.
In that case I'd recommend the Imperial. It's much cheaper than the Majestic.

2 (Example) Well, I'll be without a car . . . so I don't want to be anywhere too inconvenient.
In that case I'd recommend the Limatt. It's much more convenient than the Grand.

3 I can't stand old-fashioned hotels.
In that case I'd recommend the Hilton. It's much more modern than the Palace.

4 I don't want to be too far from the airport.
In that case I'd recommend the Skyway. It's much nearer the airport than the Bristol.

5 I have difficulty in getting to sleep at nights, so I don't want anything too noisy.
In that case I'd recommend the Lake. It's much quieter than the Imperial.

6 I don't really mind what hotel you put me in as long as it's not far from the centre.
In that case I'd recommend the Grand. It's much nearer the centre than the Limatt.

7 I'd like to stay somewhere really special. You know, not the kind of hotel that just everybody goes to.
In that case I'd recommend the Majestic. It's much more exclusive than Albert's.

8 I'm very particular about my hotel. I can't stand any dirt.
In that case I'd recommend the Grand. It's much cleaner than the Lake.

Pronunciation Practice

In this unit we're going to study two different English vowel sounds. Listen to the two examples that are given in your books.

1 *I beat him*   2 *I bit him*

Can you hear the difference between them? Which one is this?

I bit him

That was number two. Did you get that right? Now, which one is this?

I bit him

Yes, that was number two again. Now we are going to say some short sentences. Listen to the main word in these sentences, and decide whether it is like example one or example two. Write down which number you think it is. Are you ready? Listen carefully.

1 *They heat it.*   5 *What a wonderful pitch.*
2 *It's a sheep.*   6 *They're piqued.*
3 *Where's the lid?*   7 *What a feat.*
4 *Is he still leaving?*   8 *It's gin.*

Now here are the correct answers.

One was number one	Five was number two
Two was number one	Six was number one
Three was number two	Seven was number one
Four was number one	Eight was number two

How many of these did you get right? Now let's practise the pronunciation of these two sounds. Look at the little poem in your books. Poems like these are called limericks. Listen to it.

I've given the job to Miss Reed.
She is just the person I need.
She is pretty and slim
And her figure is trim
And she hits the right keys at great speed.

Did you notice how the syllables that are printed in capital letters are much longer and louder than the other ones? Now you are going to repeat this limerick line by line. Make sure you make the right difference between the vowel sounds we've been practising.

Dialogue

Mary's ringing the Skyway Hotel to book rooms for two visitors from Japan.

Receptionist: Skyway Hotel. Can I help you?

Mary Malone: This is Schweibur. I'd like to book two rooms for a Mr Takashi and a Mr Mitsui for the night of the 15th please.

Receptionist: Yes, two single rooms with bath?

Mary Malone: Yes please. And they particularly want rooms which don't face onto the main road, if that's possible.

Receptionist: Well, I'm afraid we've only got one single room on that side of the building. Unless one of the gentlemen takes a double room.

Mary Malone: Yes, I think we'd better take the single and one double in that case.

Receptionist: What were the names again, please?

Mary Malone: Mr Takashi, T-A-K-A-S-H-I, and Mr Mitsui, M-I-T-S-U-I.

Receptionist: M-I-T-S-U-I. Good. Thank you very much.

Mary Malone: Could you confirm that in writing for us, please?

Receptionist: Yes, certainly.

Mary Malone: Thank you. Goodbye.

Correspondence

In this Key suggestions for an acceptable version are printed in bold type.

Dear Mr Mouskouris,

With reference/We refer to the telephone conversation between you and Mr Gräber on May **2nd. There** appears to be a misunderstanding. Please **note** that **plans** to stop production of our XF range of **filing** cabinets **are not now going** ahead, so **there is no need/it is not necessary** for you to worry about supplying your customers. Most of our agents *(omit)* have **substantial/large** orders for this line and the customers **appear** to be satisfied with this **product**.

However, we **are still** considering whether to introduce a second range of **filing cabinets**. These would be much stronger and **more solid** than our **existing/current** range. We are *(see footnote)* doing some market research to find out what demand there would be for this new, *(omit)* improved range. Naturally, we **also want** to know the **views** of our agents. The research report will form a **basis** for discussion when you **come** to Headquarters for our next conference.

(omit)

Yours **sincerely**

Footnote In English usage *presently* would not be acceptable here and would be replaced with *at present* or *currently*. In American usage *presently* is acceptable.

Telegrams

Mary Malone is to meet a representative arriving on Garuda Flight Number 320 on Thursday.

Telegrams

Mary Malone is to cable Herr Schmidt's address in Hamburg to Mr Gräber's hotel in Paris as soon as possible.

1. GEISNER ILL STOP MEETING MUNICH FRIDAY OFF STOP CONTACT BLOCH BERLIN SOONEST STOP

2. CONFIRM PRIORITY ORDER THREE FOUR NINE ONE STOP ITEMS FOUR THREE TWO EIGHT AND FOUR THREE TWO NINE UNAVAILABLE HERE STOP TRY BRUSSELS STOP

Language Laboratory Part 2: Tapescript

Drill 3

Mary Malone works for the Assistant Manager of the Marketing Division of Schweibur. Her boss is frequently out of the office and she has to deal with a lot of telephone calls from customers in his absence.

1. (Example) Jekyll speaking; can I have a word with Mr Erich Gräber, please?
   I'm afraid Mr Gräber is out to lunch, Mr Jekyll.

2. (Example) Duclos here. Is Mr Gräber in?
   I'm afraid Mr Gräber is in a meeting, Mr Duclos.

3. Put me through to Erich, would you? It's Lebrun here.
   I'm afraid Mr Gräber is abroad this week, Mr Lebrun.

4. This is Daly from Schweibur Ireland. Is Mr Gräber there?
   I'm afraid Mr Gräber is on the other line, Mr Daly.

Now, as you will have noticed, Mary Malone isn't being very helpful to the customer. Listen to her again, when she adds a suggestion or offer of help for the customer.

1. (Example) Jekyll speaking; can I have a word with Mr Erich Gräber, please?
   I'm afraid Mr Gräber is out to lunch, Mr Jekyll. Can I take a message?

2. (Example) Duclos here. Is Mr Gräber in?
   I'm afraid Mr Gräber is in a meeting, Mr Duclos. Can I get him to call you back?

3. Put me through to Erich, would you? It's Lebrun here.
   I'm afraid Mr Gräber is abroad this week, Mr Lebrun. Can I put you through to his deputy?

4. This is Daly from Schweibur Ireland. Is Mr Gräber there?
   I'm afraid Mr Gräber is on the other line, Mr Daly. Can I ask you to call back later?

5. Hello Mary. Tell the boss that Jensen would like a moment, would you?
   I'm afraid Mr Gräber is not in the office today, Mr Jensen. Can I help at all?

6   Milewski speaking. Is Gräber at home today?
    I'm afraid Mr Gräber is showing some visitors round, Mr Milewski. Can I give him a message?

7   I'd like to speak to Mr Gräber urgently, please. Hoffmann's the name.
    I'm afraid Mr Gräber is at a conference in Gothenburg, Mr Hoffmann. Can I ask you to call 031/22 22 22?

8   Is Gräber back in circulation yet? It's Abdy speaking.
    I'm afraid Mr Gräber is still ill, Mr Abdy. Can I be of any help?

Drill 4

Mr Graber's always kept very busy at the office. Sometimes visitors who have an appointment with him have to be kept waiting for a short while because he isn't quite ready to see them.

1   (Example)   My name's Koster. I have an appointment to see Mr Gräber at three.
    Ah, good afternoon, Mr Koster. Mr Gräber is expecting you. He's just coming out of a meeting.

2   (Example)   Is this Mr Gräber's office? I arranged to see him at eleven. My name's Steiner.
    Ah, good morning, Mr Steiner. Mr Gräber is expecting you. He's just taking a phone call.

3   I've come to see Mr Gräber. Ayala's the name. Mr Gräber said he would be free at nine thirty.
    Ah, good morning, Mr Ayala. Mr Gräber is expecting you. He's just dealing with an unexpected enquiry.

4   I'm Nilsson. I've an appointment with Mr Gräber at ten.
    Ah, good morning, Mr Nilsson. Mr Gräber is expecting you. He's just checking up on the terms of the contract.

If a visitor has to be kept waiting like this, as a matter of politeness the secretary should ask him to sit down and reassure him that he will not be kept waiting long.

1   (Example)   My name's Koster. I have an appointment to see Mr Gräber at three.
    Ah, good afternoon, Mr Koster. Mr Gräber is expecting you. He's just coming out of a meeting. If you'd care to take a seat, he'll be with you in a moment.

2   (Example)   Is this Mr Gräber's office? I arranged to see him at eleven. My name's Steiner.
    Ah, good morning, Mr Steiner. Mr Gräber is expecting you. He's just taking a phone call. If you'd care to take a seat, he won't keep you waiting long.

Language Laboratory Part 2

3   I've come to see Mr Gräber. Ayala's the name. Mr Gräber said he would be free at nine thirty.
    Ah, good morning, Mr Ayala. Mr Gräber is expecting you. He's just dealing with an unexpected enquiry. If you'd care to take a seat, he won't be more than a few minutes.

4   I'm Nilsson. I've an appointment with Mr Gräber at ten.
    Ah, good morning, Mr Nilsson. Mr Gräber is expecting you. He's just checking up on the terms of the contract. If you'd care to take a seat, he'll be with you shortly.

5   Good afternoon. May I see Mr Gräber? I have an appointment. My name's Johnson.
    Ah, good afternoon, Mr Johnson. Mr Gräber is expecting you. He's just showing out his last visitor. If you'd care to take a seat, he'll be back directly.

6   I think my secretary made an appointment for me to see Mr Gräber today, at eleven thirty. The name's Post.
    Ah, good morning, Mr Post. Mr Gräber is expecting you. He's just finishing a briefing session. If you'd care to take a seat, he'll be free in a minute.

7   I promised to come and see Mr Gräber this afternoon. Lamartine's the name.
    Ah, good afternoon, Mr Lamartine. Mr Gräber is expecting you. He's just attending to an urgent matter. If you'd care to take a seat, he won't be long.

8   My name's de Freitas. I've an appointment with Mr Gräber at four.
    Ah, good afternoon, Mr de Freitas. Mr Gräber is expecting you. He's just talking to one of the directors. If you'd care to take a seat, he'll be ready to see you in a minute.

Active Listening

Passage 1: Your boss, the Training Manager, has dictated a letter onto a dictation machine.

Dear Sir,

Er, this is the heading, so underline it: Training in Switzerland for Mr I Achebe. Then: Thank you for your letter of 1st May. Para.

I regret that we have had, no, cancel that, I regret to have to inform you that we have had to cancel our courses scheduled for June, due to lack of interest from our various field organizations. Para.

We will, however, still be able to arrange an adequate training programme for Mr Achebe, provided that he is willing to study on his own for part of the time. This private study would, of course, be under the supervision of one of our quality supervisors. We suggest that he arrives on, er, the, er,

May 5th, and stays for twelve weeks, leaving at the end of, er, Week 32. Para.

These twelve weeks would be mainly taken up by theoretical training. For practical training, if required, we usually rely on our companies abroad. Should Mr Achebe need further training on, for example, testing, no cancel that last sentence, and start again as follows: Perhaps you could let us know as soon as possible whether Mr Achebe requires such further training on, for example, testing, so that we can make the necessary arrangements. Para.

Could you please send us the particulars about Mr Achebe that we require by completing the enclosed Proposal Form. I assume that you would like us to arrange his accommodation, and that he'll be receiving the usual allowances etc given to participants on our regular courses. Para.

We look forward to hearing from you shortly.

Yours sincerely, and that's for my signature.

1. What were the last two words you heard?
   Dear Sir

2. What are you to do?
   underline the heading

3. What were the last three words you heard?
   to have to

4. What were the last two words you heard?
   due to

5. What were the last three words you heard?
   on his own

6. What was the last word you heard?
   our

7. Did that last sound have any meaning or not?
   no

8. What were the last two words you heard?
   requires such

9. What was the last word you heard?
   etc/etcetera

Passage 2: Mary Malone received the following telephone call one morning. Her boss, Mr Gräber, was out.

Mary Malone: Good morning, Mr Gräber's office. Can I help you?

Daly: Good morning, Daly speaking. I'd like to speak to Mr Erich Gräber, if I may.

Mary Malone: I'm afraid Mr Gräber won't be in the office till this afternoon. Can I help at all?

Daly: Oh, that's a pity. I wonder if you could give him a message from me. Tell him that I accept immediately all but two of the points in his letter, and that would be numbers three, no hang on, where are we, ah, here we are, one, two, three, four and seven, no ten, which I'd like him to clarify, and that if he could call me back as soon as he returns, I'd be most grateful. I'm not in the office, I'm in London, so could he ring 01-330-4445. Did you get all that?

Mary Malone: Yes, Mr Daly, I'll tell Mr Gräber as soon as he gets back.

Daly: Thank you so much. Goodbye.

Mary Malone: Goodbye, Mr Daly, and thank you.

1. How many points in Mr Gräber's letter has Mr Daly not accepted immediately?
   Two

2. Which points were they?
   Four and ten

3. What does Mr Daly want Mr Gräber to do?
   He wants him to clarify these two points

4. What number did Mr Daly give?
   01-330-4445

5. Now write out the message you would give Mr Gräber on his return.
   Mr Daly phoned to say that he accepts all the points in your letter except Nos. 4 and 10. He would like you to clarify these. Please ring him at London 01-330-4445

Role Simulation

Situation

The students are asked to imagine that they have been detailed to act as guides for a group of visitors on a conducted tour of their company. Their task is to answer the visitors' questions. As far as possible, the students should be encouraged to imagine it is their own company they are talking about.

Preparation

In order to answer the visitors' questions they must be in possession of the facts about their company and should be asked to find out beforehand about such things as number of employees, annual turnover, range of products, etc.

Procedure

The students take it in turn to play the part of secretary/guide.

They should:
1. welcome the visitors to the company
2. introduce themselves
3. offer to answer any questions the visitors may have about the company
4. respond to any comment the visitors might make.

Students should also be given a copy of one of the visitor's roles given below. These consist of a question and a comment to put to the secretary/guide. It is left to the discretion of the teacher as to how many questions the secretary/guide should be required to answer before the next pupil is appointed to the leading role.

Visitors' Roles

1. I wonder if you can tell me roughly how many people work for . . . ?
   I didn't realize you employed so many/few people.

2. I'd be interested to know what the annual turnover of the Company/Group is.
   It must be an expanding business.

3. Could you tell me something about the history of the Company?
   You must find it very interesting working here.

4. Who's at the head of the Company? You know, the Chief Executive.
   I don't suppose he makes all the decisions himself.

5. I'm not entirely clear how many different product lines you have.
   I'd be interested to see how you . . ./how . . . works.

6. How is the Company organized? Is it divided into sections or departments?
   I don't suppose you ever get to know what goes on in the other sections/departments.

7. Do you export many of your goods?
   There must/ought to be quite a big demand for . . . overseas.

8. Does the Company run any training programmes for the staff?
   I'd quite like to know more about the kind of courses you run.

9. You speak English very well. Do you have to use English a lot in your job?
   It must be quite difficult to understand all the different accents.

10. Does the Company provide any facilities for the staff? Is there a canteen?
    I imagine a lot of the staff use/make use of the . . .

Key to 'What is this?'

Page 4: paper clip
Page 5: stapling machine
Page 6: filing cabinet
Page 15: file, wallet file, ring binder

Unit 2

Unit Summary

Introductory Recording	This episode is entitled 'The Sales Report'. In it Mary Malone is asked to phone up one of Schweibur's subsidiaries to enquire about a sales report that has not turned up and to get information for her boss, Mr Gräber.
Text	The Text is the Sales Report referred to in the Introductory Recording.
Vocabulary	Exercise A is a three-part exercise on vocabulary which appears in the Text.
Structures	1 Present perfect/past simple (Exercise B and Drill 1) We *haven't signed* the contract yet. My stapler *broke* yesterday. 2 The use of intensifiers and modifiers (Exercise C and Drill 2) The food is *rather* good.
Pronunciation Practice	This deals with the difference between the vowel sounds [e] as in *pet* and [æ] as in *pat*. There is an ear-training exercise followed by repetition of a limerick.
Dialogue	The situation is that of dealing with a complaint from a customer.
Correspondence	There is a draft letter to be corrected.
Telegrams	There are four telegrams: two to be decoded and two to be encoded.
Gambits	Drill 3: Insisting. *I'm afraid . . . really must be . . . , otherwise . . .* Drill 4: Asking for repetition. *Sorry, I didn't get that . . . . Did you say . . . ?*
Active Listening	There are three passages in this unit. 1 A telephone conversation giving instructions. The student has to answer comprehension questions. 2 A telephone message which the students have to write down. 3 Comprehension of a recorded instruction.
Role Simulation	The students are asked to imagine that their boss has been delayed for an

appointment with a visitor. Their task is to receive the visitor and engage him in conversation. The students act out this Role Simulation in pairs; one student playing the role of secretary, the other the role of visitor. Roles are provided for the students.

Homework

The written gambits introduced in this unit deal with:

Drawing attention and reminding
Expressing urgency and necessity
Expressing willingness and offers of help

Additional Notes

Exercise C

This is an oral exercise practising the use of intensifiers and modifiers. It is designed to lead from simple responses to more open-ended discussion.

Step 1: The students take it in turn to play the parts of Mary Malone and Miss Keller, using the tables provided.

Step 2: Ask the class what they would recommend a visitor to see and do in their town. Put a list up on the blackboard.

Step 3: Now get the students to imagine that they are talking to a visitor. Get them to make sentences with the following patterns:

I would recommend . . .   *It's/They're extremely . . .*
I wouldn't recommend . . .   *It's/They're somewhat . . .*

Introductory Recording

Tapescript

Erich Gräber is the Assistant Marketing Manager of Schweibur International, a group of companies producing office equipment. This morning he is in his office in Zurich, attending to routine matters with the help of his personal secretary, Mary Malone. Mr Gräber has been waiting for a sales report to arrive from Andersen's, an associate company in Copenhagen.

Gräber: Now, Mary, has that report arrived?

Malone: Which report, Mr Gräber?

Gräber: You know, the monthly sales report we've been waiting for—from Copenhagen. I'm rather anxious. It was due on Monday.

Malone: Well, it hasn't arrived, I'm sure.

Gräber: Oh, dear. Look, could I ask you to ring Pedersen in Copenhagen. Make it about ten. He's never in before then.

Malone: Right, Mr Gräber. A bit after ten.

Introductory Recording

Gräber: Thanks. It really is extremely important to get this report. My own report is due at three this afternoon. And I especially need the information on . . . *(Fade)*

Pedersen: Allo. Pedersen.

Malone: Oh, Mr Pedersen, good morning. This is Schweibur, Zurich. Mary Malone, Mr Gräber's secretary. He asked me to ring you about your sales report. He rather expected it to arrive this morning.

Pedersen: Ah yes, Miss Malone. Kind of you to ring. The report has been posted, I'm sure. Erm, my deputy Niels Olsen prepared it. I've just been talking to him, in fact. Look, shall I get you transferred to him?

Malone: Oh, yes, thank you, Mr Pedersen . . .

Olsen: Olsen.

Malone: Oh, good morning, Mr Olsen. It's Mary Malone, Mr Gräber's secretary speaking. He asked me to ring you, er, to check up on the monthly sales report. He's a bit worried. He expected it to arrive on Monday.

Olsen: Oh. Oh, yes. Good morning, Miss Malone. Yes, that report. I posted it last night. At about eight o'clock, you know.

Malone: Well, I'm afraid it hasn't arrived yet.

Olsen: Well, um, it was sent a bit late, I suppose. I had some difficulty myself, in actually getting the information from the branches and agents here in Denmark, you see. Had to drive, oh, about two hundred kilometres to one branch on Friday and back again, of course. Didn't get home until after ten. Then I worked all day Saturday. It was all rather tiring.

Malone: Yes, I see. Well, . . .

Olsen: But I put it in the post myself. Yesterday. About eight o'clock.

Malone: That's fine. But there were one or two particular items Mr Gräber wanted me to check with you.

Olsen: You mean items in the report?

Malone: Yes, that's right, Mr Olsen.

Olsen: Ah, erm, but can't they wait until the report arrives?

Malone: But what if it doesn't arrive today? You only posted it yesterday. And, anyway, his own report is due at three this afternoon. So it really is extremely . . .

Olsen: OK, OK. Erm, what is it you want to know?

Malone: First, sales of the Verso filing system.

Olsen: Yes, the Verso. Can I just look at my notes? Yes, well, this is their third month. Sales fell in the first week, but recovered very well, um, rather more than the previous best total, in fact. 327 units in the month.

Malone: I'm sorry, Mr Olsen, I didn't quite catch that figure.

Olsen: 327 units for the month, 327.

Malone: Oh, thank you. And he wanted to know which outlets have done best in these sales.

Olsen: Well, Copenhagen's done extremely well, of course. 130 units sold. And Odense, with . . .

Malone: Sorry, Mr Olsen, could you spell that for me?

Olsen: Odense? Yes, of course. O-D-E-N-S-E. Got that?

Malone: N-S-E. Yes, thank you.

Olsen: So, Odense 85 units. And Aarhus 80. OK?

Malone: Yes, fine. Thank you.

Olsen: Good. Anything else?

Malone: Er, no, nothing else. Thank you very much, Mr Olsen.

Olsen: That's OK. And you'll get the report very soon of course.

Malone: Yes, I hope so. Goodbye for now, Mr Olsen. Goodbye.

Olsen: OK. Goodbye.

Comprehension Questions

1. Why is Mr Gräber rather worried?
   A sales report that he is expecting has not yet arrived.

2. Where is this report from?
   Copenhagen.

3. Why does he ask Mary Malone to phone about it?
   Because he needs the information in this report urgently (so that he can write his own report).

4. The first person Mary speaks to on the phone is a Mr Pedersen. What does he do?
   He transfers the call to his deputy (Mr Olsen) who wrote the report.

5. Has the report been sent off?
   Yes, Mr Olsen posted it the previous night.

6. Mr Olsen was rather late in sending off this report. What has he got to say about that?
   He makes excuses. (He explains that he had difficulty in getting the information.)

Introductory Recording

7 Can you remember what sort of product Mr Gräber wanted information about?
A filing system. (The Verso filing system.)

8 What is the first thing Mr Gräber wants to know about it?
What the sales were like this month.

9 What other piece of information does he want?
Which places sold most of these filing systems.

10 What town was in second position after Copenhagen?
Odense.

Text: The Sales Report

The words and phrases in italics are quoted verbatim from the Text.

Comprehension Questions

1 What has been put in the box at the top of the report?
The *code number*.

2 Did the Verso filing system do well in the first week of May?
No, it didn't. *Sales dropped slightly*.

3 Did sales continue to fall?
No, they didn't. They *recovered well*.

4 What does the figure 327 represent?
It represents *the number of units sold in Denmark as a whole*.

5 How did the May sales compare with the April sales?
There was *an increase of 41 units over the previous month*.

6 What does this show?
It *shows a satisfactory upward trend in sales of this product*.

7 Apart from the units sold through the principal outlets, another 15 units were sold. How?
They were sold as a result of enquiries direct to Schweibur's export department.

8 Why did the writer visit all the agents?
To get information so that he could *estimate sales for the third quarter*.

9 What does Jürgens think of the Verso system?
He *has already expressed his enthusiasm for the new range*.

10 What does he think of the sales prospects for the Verso?
He *is completely confident that he can maintain high sales*.

11 What does he think about competition for the product?
He feels Schweibur is *now ahead in this field as far as the Danish market is concerned*.

12 What did the writer decide on with the agent?
    They *decided on a provisional sales target*.

13 What was the figure of 450 based on?
    It was based on Schweibur's *scheduled production figures and an analysis of the state of the market*.

14 Is the 200 units that Jürgens is going to receive in June his whole quota?
    No, it isn't. It's only the *first instalment of his allocation*.

15 What has Jürgens agreed to do?
    He *has agreed to submit a report on customer reaction to the new range*.

16 What is Nilsson's reaction to the new range?
    He *is also very positive*.

17 Has he had good sales?
    Yes, *he sold many more units than he anticipated*.

18 What would he like to do as a result of these high sales?
    He would like to increase his quota from 100 to 120 units in the coming quarter.

19 What did Nilsson complain about?
    He complained that Schweibur frequently did not give him sufficient notice of proposed price increases.

20 What assurance did the writer give him?
    He *assured him that in future* Schweibur would *notify him sooner of any changes*.

21 What further action must the writer take?
    He must *check up on the revised quota with Production*.

22 Does Christiansen stock the Verso system?
    Not yet. But he has ordered 10 units for the next quarter.

23 What does Christiansen think about the new range?
    He expressed the opinion that the Verso system was rather expensive (especially for the type of customer in his area).

24 What was Christiansen worried about?
    He was *anxious about the future of the old Fileasy system*.

Key to the Exercises

Exercise A

1 A number of units were sold as a result of *enquiries* from customers.
2 The company has to *estimate* how many units it will sell.
3 I'm afraid some of the agents don't *stock* the Verso system.
4 A number of agents have *expressed* an opinion on the new range.
5 We have based this on our *scheduled* production figures.

Key to the Exercises 33

6   We should *notify* agents of any price increases.
7   Copenhagen is one of the *principal outlets*.
8   We are satisfied with the *upward trend* in sales.
9   450 was the figure agreed on as the *sales target*.
10 It would be interesting to know the *customer reaction* to the new range.
11 We are extremely proud of this design and are *confident* that sales will be high.
12 Customers are satisfied with the product so it should be easy to *maintain* high sales.
13 We cannot deliver the whole order this month but we can let you have the first *instalment*.
14 We have not yet reached a final decision so this figure is only *provisional*.
15 We have overspent our *budget* by more than 5,000 dollars.

Exercise B

1   We sent off those invoices yesterday afternoon.
2   I have just transferred the call to the Training Department.
3   I can't find my entry pass. Have you seen it anywhere?
4   I paid this account last week but they still haven't sent a receipt.
5   This is the second time this week that the photocopier has broken down.
6   Did you catch what he said?
7   I refunded their expenses a few days ago.
8   We have never had a crisis like this in the office before.
9   His letter came last week and we answered it by return.
10 Look what they have done! They have sent us the wrong size of manilla envelopes. I ordered giant size ones.

Exercise C

As this is an open-ended exercise, no key can be provided.

Language Laboratory Part 1: Tapescript

Drill 1

Mr Konstanz, who is the Training Manager at Schweibur, is rather forgetful, and he always leaves things until the last moment. Luckily, his secretary, Miss Miller, is very efficient.

1   (Example)   Have you typed up the report yet, Miss Miller?
    I typed it up this morning.

2   (Example)   We'd better circulate it then.
    I've already circulated it.

3   But was everybody notified about the meeting?
    I notified them three weeks ago.

4   And what about booking the room?
    I booked it last week.

5   Fine. The next thing is to settle those invoices.
    I've just this moment settled them.

	6	And could you send off those brochures? *I sent them off on Monday.*
	7	Oh, good lord! I haven't fixed up that appointment. *I've already fixed it up.*
	8	And I asked you to book my theatre tickets. You didn't forget, did you? *I booked them yesterday.*

Drill 2

Miss Miller is talking to a visitor, a Mr Mucha, who is waiting to see her boss.

1 (Example) Travelling by air is somewhat tiring, I always think.
   Yes, it is rather tiring.

2 (Example) It's very difficult to get a taxi at the airport.
   Yes, it is extremely difficult.

3 (Example) Having to wait for buses is a little inconvenient, isn't it?
   Yes, it is a bit inconvenient.

4 It's quite cold for the time of year.
   Yes, it is rather cold.

5 I understand Mr Schranz's illness is very serious.
   Yes, it is extremely serious.

6 It feels a little too warm in here, don't you think?
   Yes, it is a bit too warm.

7 The office seems fairly busy today, I must say.
   Yes, it is rather busy.

8 These meetings are a little unsatisfactory.
   Yes, they are a bit unsatisfactory.

Pronunciation Practice

In this unit we're going to study another two English vowel sounds. Listen to the two example words that are given in your book.

1 *pet*

2 *pat*

Can you hear the difference between them? Which one is this?
pet

That was number one. Which one is this?
pat

That was number two. Which one is this?
pat

That was number two again. Now we're going to say ten words. Write down whether the word has the same sound as example one or example two.

Language Laboratory Part 1

Are you ready? Listen carefully.

1	*mesh*	6	*tan*
2	*peck*	7	*fad*
3	*bad*	8	*gem*
4	*ate*	9	*send*
5	*ben*	10	*patch*

Now here are the correct answers.

One was number one	Six was number two
Two was number one	Seven was number two
Three was number two	Eight was number one
Four was number one	Nine was number one
Five was number one	Ten was number two

How many of these did you get right? Well, don't worry if your score wasn't a hundred per cent. Nearly everybody finds these two sounds particularly difficult. Now let's practise the pronunciation of the two sounds. Look at the limerick in your book. Listen to it first.

This report is most pressing, Miss Matchett;
Send this letter as well and attach it.
But he left no address,
And so to her distress,
The poor secretary couldn't dispatch it.

Now repeat this limerick line by line. Remember that the syllables that are printed in capitals in your book are much louder and longer than the others. And try to make some difference between the two example vowel sounds.

Dialogue

Mr Gräber, Schweibur's Assistant Marketing Manager, is out of the office when a customer rings to complain about a delayed order. Mary Malone deals with the complaint.

Rivelini: Hallo?

Malone: Mr Gräber's office.

Rivelini: Can I speak to the Assistant Marketing Manager, please?

Malone: I'm afraid Mr Gräber isn't in at the moment. Can I help you at all?

Rivelini: Yes, my name's Rivelini from IMP, Milan. I was promised delivery of 500 PBXs a week ago, and they still haven't arrived.

Malone: I'm sorry to hear that, Mr Rivelini.

Rivelini: You sent an invoice, though, and I'm certainly not going to pay it until I get the goods.

Malone: Naturally not, Mr Rivelini. Could you give me the invoice number?

Rivelini: PB 3856.

Malone: Thank you. I'll ask Mr Gräber to look into the matter as soon as I can get hold of him.

Rivelini: And please tell him we need those units urgently.

Malone: Of course. I'm very sorry there's been a delay.

Rivelini: You'll ring me back later this afternoon, then?

Malone: Yes, of course, as soon as we can.

Rivelini: Right. I look forward to hearing from you. Goodbye.

Malone: Goodbye, Mr Rivelini.

Correspondence

In this Key suggestions for an acceptable version are printed in bold type.

Dear Sir/Gentlemen

This **is** the third month that your **monthly** sales report **has reached us** late. In fact, **it has arrived later** and **later**.

This month it **arrived** on 12th, which is two weeks **later** than it should have **done**. Not only that, but the figures you háve **given** me are **more inadequate** than ever. I **notice, for example**, that you **have recorded** sales of the **Schweibur** year planner as a question mark. This **does not help** very much when I review overall sales **within the** group.

Would you be **so** kind as to supply **more detailed/complete** information in the future, under the headings **I have indicated** in the enclosed outline.

Yours faithfully/sincerely,

Telegrams

We confirm that we have received two of item 24675/AB. Consignment number 453/S has been delayed due to a strike.

1. HOLD EVERYTHING PENDING MY ARRIVAL ROME FOURTEEN FIFTEEN THIS SATURDAY

2. SEND FOUR OF H STROKE THIRTY FOUR STROKE C ASAP STOP URGENT

Language Laboratory Part 2: Tapescript

Drill 3

Inge Lindfors is Mr Karlberger's secretary. It's up to her to see that things get done. Sometimes people tell her that they can't do something, and very often she has to insist that it must be done.

1. (Example) Ah, Mrs Lindfors, about your indent for two packets of giant size manilla envelopes. I doubt whether we can deliver these today. Would tomorrow be OK?
I'm afraid the envelopes really must be delivered today.

2. (Example) Look here, Inge, I've just had a note from Karlberger bringing forward the date of the next meeting. This is really most inconvenient. Why can't we keep it as it was?
I'm afraid the date of the next meeting really must be brought forward.

3. Look, Inge, I don't think I can submit those estimates to Mr Karlberger by tomorrow. Is that going to cause a crisis?
I'm afraid the estimates really must be submitted by tomorrow.

4. Mrs Lindfors, I'm sorry to have to tell you that we may not be able to repair the photocopier before next week. I hope that won't inconvenience you too much.
I'm afraid the photocopier really must be repaired before next week.

Now, when Mrs Lindfors insists that something must be done she usually gives the person some reason for her insistence. If she did not, she would sound too abrupt.

1. (Example) Ah, Mrs Lindfors, about your indent for two packets of giant size manilla envelopes. I doubt whether we can deliver these today. Would tomorrow be OK?
I'm afraid the envelopes really must be delivered today, otherwise the conference brochures won't be mailed.

2. (Example) Look here, Inge, I've just had a note from Karlberger bringing forward the date of the next meeting. This is really most inconvenient. Why can't we keep it as it was?
I'm afraid the date of the next meeting really must be brought forward, otherwise the contracts won't be drafted in time.

3. Look, Inge, I don't think I can submit those estimates to Mr Karlberger by tomorrow. Is that going to cause a crisis?
I'm afraid the estimates really must be submitted by tomorrow, otherwise the budget won't be drawn up in time.

4. Mrs Lindfors, I'm sorry to have to tell you that we may not be able to repair the photocopier before next week. I hope that won't inconvenience you too much.
I'm afraid the photocopier really must be repaired before next week, otherwise the quarterly report won't be circulated.

5 Inge, I can't find my hotel receipts. Does it really matter if I don't include them?
I'm afraid your hotel receipts really must be included, otherwise your expenses won't be refunded.

6 Is that you, Inge? Gunther here. It's about my trip to France. Do we really have to settle the dates by Friday? I haven't quite made up my mind yet.
I'm afraid the dates really must be settled by Friday, otherwise your hotel rooms won't be booked.

7 Inge, it's Maureen here. Do I really have to type the code number on every page? It does seem to be such a waste of time.
I'm afraid the code number really must be typed on every page, otherwise the papers won't be filed correctly.

8 I've lost my entry pass, Inge. Get another one for me, will you? I haven't bothered to report the loss, by the way.
I'm afraid the loss really must be reported, otherwise a new pass won't be issued.

Drill 4

Schweibur, Zurich, has a rather inefficient internal telephone system and there is often interference on the line. When that happens Mrs Lindfors has to ask somebody to repeat a piece of information that she hasn't understood.

1 (Example) Mr Karlberger is going to *(interference)* tomorrow.
Sorry, I didn't get that. Where did you say he was going?

2 (Example) Two representatives from GKB are coming next *(interference)*.
Sorry, I didn't get that. When did you say they were coming?

3 Mr *(interference)* is arranging the meeting.
Sorry, I didn't get that. Who did you say was arranging the meeting?

4 They're staying at the *(interference)* hotel.
Sorry, I didn't get that. Where did you say they were staying?

5 Mr *(interference)* is the Technical Director.
Sorry, I didin't get that. Who did you say was the Technical Director?

6 We pay them *(interference)* francs for their services.
Sorry, I didn't get that. How much did you say we paid them?

7 Mr *(interference)* has the figures.
Sorry, I didn't get that. Who did you say had the figures?

8 What Miss Lacheral will be doing is to *(interference)*.
Sorry, I didn't get that. What did you say she would be doing?

Active Listening

Passage 1: Mrs Lindfors had the following telephone conversation with her boss recently, the day after he had left for Paris.

Language Laboratory Part 2

Mrs Lindfors: Mr Karlberger's office.

Karlberger: Ah, good morning, Mrs Lindfors. Karlberger here. I'm afraid I've done something rather stupid. I've left some important papers behind that I should have brought with me. Could you send them on to me straight away?

Mrs Lindfors: Yes, of course, Mr Karlberger.

Karlberger: They're in a brown folder marked BCG Paris, which I rather think is lying on my desk, but if it isn't there it'll be on the top shelf of the cupboard in my office.

Mrs Lindfors: Don't worry. I'll find it.

Karlberger: And could you get that off immediately, express please, to my hotel here. The address is in the file.

Mrs Lindfors: Anything else, Mr Karlberger?

Karlberger: No, that's all, thank you. Goodbye.

Mrs Lindfors: Goodbye.

1. What has Mr Karlberger left behind?
   Some important papers.

2. What does he want Mrs Lindfors to do?
   Send them on to him straight away.

3. How will Mrs Lindfors recognize the folder?
   It's marked BCG Paris.

4. Where does Mr Karlberger think the folder is?
   Lying on his desk.

5. If it's not there, where will it be?
   On the top shelf of the cupboard in his office.

6. How does Mr Karlberger want the folder sent?
   By express.

Passage 2: Mrs Lindfors had the following telephone conversation with Mr Maier, who was calling from Schweibur's branch in Geneva.

Mrs Lindfors: Mr Karlberger's office, can I help you?

Maier: Mrs Lindfors?

Mrs Lindfors: Yes, speaking.

Maier: It's Maier, from Schweibur, Geneva, here. Can you give Karlberger a message when he gets back tomorrow? The engineer he left in Geneva this morning on that maintenance job has fallen down and broken his leg, the damned fool! Could he please send a replacement as soon as possible, and telephone the customer, he'll know which customer, to let them know who's coming and when. I shan't be in the office tomorrow, but could he let Stein know what's been fixed. Got that?

Mrs Lindfors: Yes, I'll tell him first thing in the morning, Mr Maier.

Maier: Splendid. 'Bye.

Mrs Lindfors: Goodbye, Mr Maier.

What is the message Mr Maier wants given to Mr Karlberger?
Mr Maier rang to say that the engineer in Geneva has broken his leg. Could you send a replacement as soon as possible and inform the customer who is coming and when. Could you let Mr Stein know tomorrow what has been arranged.

Passage 3: Before he went to Paris, your boss recorded the following message for you.

On my desk you'll find three draft letters. Could you get them off as soon as poss, sending the German and Dutch ones by express, but not the one to Spain.

What do you have to do?
Send off the three letters as soon as possible. Send the letters to Germany and Holland by express, and the one to Spain by ordinary mail.

Role Simulation

Situation

The students are asked to imagine that their boss has been delayed for an appointment with a visitor. Their task is to receive the visitor and engage him in conversation. The students should first agree on a name for the boss. They should act out their roles as though they were in their own company.

Procedure

The students should act out this Role Simulation in pairs; one student playing the role of secretary, the other the role of visitor. Each student should be given a copy of one of the following roles.

The 'visitors' should
1 begin by introducing themselves
2 respond to the secretary's conversation 'openers'
3 ask questions as shown in the role card.

The 'secretaries' should
1 greet the visitor
2 explain the delay
3 start up a conversation
4 answer any questions the visitors may have.

Role Simulation

Roles

1. **Visitor:** You are an Argentinian. Invent a name and a position for yourself. Begin by explaining who you are and why you have come. In answer to the secretary's questions: this is the first time you have been to her country. Make some polite comment about the country, and remark on something you find particularly interesting. You are staying for a week, and will have some free time. Ask what she thinks you should try and see.

   Secretary: Greet the visitor and explain the delay (urgent phone call). Offer to take his coat. Ask if this is his first visit to your country and if he is enjoying it. Ask how long he is staying. Answer his questions.

2. **Visitor:** You are a German. Invent a name and a position for yourself. Begin by asking if you've got the right office then introduce yourself. Accept the cup of coffee she offers. In reply to her question: you are here for a week for a series of meetings. Name the hotel you're staying in. Make one favourable comment about it and then say that it is too far from the company offices for convenience. Also list a number of small complaints. Ask her if she can recommend another hotel.

   Secretary: Greet the visitor and explain the delay (car has broken down). Offer him a cup of coffee (don't forget to ask about milk and sugar). Find out whether he is staying with someone in the company or at a hotel. Ask if the accommodation is satisfactory. Answer his questions.

3. **Visitor:** You are a Norwegian. Invent a name and a position for yourself. Begin by explaining who you are and apologize for being late for the appointment. Decline the offer of a cup of coffee (give a reason). In reply to the secretary's questions: you had no difficulty finding the building but got on the wrong bus. Ask her to explain the best way to get back to the centre of town by public transport.

   Secretary: Greet the visitor and explain the delay (meeting going on longer than expected). Offer him a cup of coffee. Ask him if he had difficulty in finding the office. Say you were worried the directions you gave him were not clear enough. Answer his questions.

4. **Visitor:** You are an Indian. Invent a name and a position for yourself. Begin by asking for the boss, then explain who you are and why you are here. Refuse the offer of magazines (give a reason). In reply to the secretary's questions: you have been here several times before. You are going to have lunch with her boss, you like European food. Ask her if she ever travels abroad and if she has thought of going to India.

   Secretary: Greet visitors and explain the delay (dealing with an urgent query). Offer him some magazines to read. Ask him if he will be having lunch here and whether he has any special diet. Answer his questions.

5 **Visitor:** You are an Englishman. Invent a name and a position for yourself. Begin by explaining who you are and why you are here. When you hear of the delay, ask how long you will have to wait and whether there would be enough time to go to the shops. In reply to the secretary's questions, explain that you would like to buy a present for your wife. Ask her to suggest something that would be typical of her country.

Secretary: Greet the visitor and explain the delay (called to the Managing Director's office). Will be back very shortly. Ask him if there is anything you can get for him. Find out about his family and answer his questions.

Key to 'What is this?'

Page 21: drawing pins.
Page 25: hole punch
Page 26: directory and telephone

Unit Summary 43

Unit 3

Unit Summary

Introductory Recording This episode is entitled 'The Thanking Letter'. In it Erich Gräber outlines a thanking letter that he would like Mary Malone to write for him.

Text The Text is the thanking letter that Mary Malone drafted for Gräber.

Vocabulary Exercise A is a three-part exercise on vocabulary which appears in the Text.

Structures
1 Future tenses
   a Present continuous, when used for a definite future arrangement (Drills 1 and 2)
      He's *arriving* at one o'clock.
   b Future continuous, when used to imply an action that will occur in the normal course of events (Exercise B)
      He'll *be leaving* tomorrow.
   c Future simple, when used for a formal/neutral reference to future events (Exercise B and Drill 1)
      The meeting *will last* an hour.

2 Prepositions of time
   At, in, on (Exercise C and Drill 2)
   At five o'clock
   In the morning
   On Sunday

Pronunciation Practice This deals with the difference between the vowel sounds [ɑ] as in *lark*, [o] as in *lock* and [ʌ] as in *luck*. There is an ear-training exercise followed by repetition of a limerick.

Dialogue The situation is that of making an appointment.

Correspondence There is a draft letter to be corrected.

Telegrams There are four telegrams, two to be decoded and two to be encoded.

Gambits Drill 3: Relaying abrupt messages politely.
I'm afraid Mr Karlberger is . . . , Mr . . . . Would . . . be convenient?

Drill 4: Offering to help.
Perhaps I can help you. Shall I . . . for you?

Active Listening		There are three passages in this unit.
	1	A telephone message. The students have to answer comprehension questions.
	2	A telephone message. The students have to write down the message.
	3	Comprehension of a recorded instruction.

Role Simulation

In this unit the students are asked to imagine that an employee from one of their company's overseas branches is attending a six-week training course at their company. Their task is to answer his questions and to give him such help as they can.

The teacher is asked to take the part of the foreign employee. Guidelines are provided for the teacher.

Homework

The written gambits introduced in the unit deal with:

Apologizing and expressing regret
Giving assurances
Asking for clarification

Additional Notes

Exercise C

This is an oral exercise practising the prepositions of time *at*, *in* and *on*. It is in two parts, the first part dealing with the normal use of these prepositions, the second with some of the commoner exceptions.

Step 1: The teacher should take the part of Mr Boileau, who is trying to arrange a time to see Mr Shermann with his secretary, Miss Jones. The students should take it in turns to be Miss Jones.

Start by asking the first student whether you can see Mr Shermann at a particular time when he is busy (cf Shermann's diary). Make sure that you use the prepositions the exercise is practising!

(Example)   Can I see Shermann *at* ten *in* the morning *on* 19th?

Get the student to respond, making sure that she suggests an alternative time to the one you asked for.

The teacher can lengthen the practice given to any one student by refusing the time she suggests, and asking for a second time that he knows Mr Shermann would not be available.

(Example)   Can I see Shermann *at* ten *in* the morning *on* 19th?
No, Mr Shermann has a meeting *in the morning*. What about ten o'clock *in the morning* on 21st?
No that's no good. Can I come *at* ten *on* Thursday?

I'm afraid Mr Jenkins is coming at *ten. Would two thirty* on *Thursday afternoon be convenient?*
etc.

Step 2: When the normal use of these prepositions has been established, move on to the gap exercise where some of the other uses are practised.

Introductory Recording

Tapescript

The Thanking Letter
It is first thing in the morning. The offices of Schweibur International in Zurich have just opened. Erich Gräber, Assistant Marketing Manager, who was on a visit to Canada last week, is back in his office.

Malone: Yes, Mr Gräber?

Gräber: Good morning, Mary. Er, look, I've got a letter to write. It's a bit difficult, and, er, . . .

Malone: Perhaps I can help you, Mr Gräber. Shall I come in?

Gräber: Oh, yes, please. And better make it right away. I'm going to see Hoffmann at ten.

Malone: I'll be right in.

Gräber: Good. Now, this letter. You know I went to Canada last week. For the regional planning conference.

Malone: Yes, of course. Oh, and by the way, you asked me to remind you to write to . . .

Gräber: Exactly. That's what you're going to help me with. The thank-you letter to Jim. I'm not very good at that sort of thing. And I want to get it just right.

Malone: Yes, Mr Gräber. How can I help?

Gräber: Well, take notes and write them up as a proper letter afterwards. OK? Good. Er, well, let's see. It's to Jim Harris. You'll find the address in my book. So. Dear Jim to start. Then something about my wife and I stopping off in Montreal at the weekend on our way back. We liked it very much, as he said we would. Fascinating city.

Malone: Erm, did Mr Harris suggest the visit to you?

Gräber: Yes, it was his idea. So some sort of thank you for that. And, para. Um, now, the planning conference. It was the first of its kind but it was a great success. This was mainly due to his efforts, and I'm extremely grateful. And, er, I'm sure it was very valuable for the people taking part. And I hope these conferences will become a regular event throughout the Schweibur group. Got that?

Malone: Yes, that's fine.

Gräber: Now. Yes, and you could mention to Jim that in fact I'm going to Lagos in July to make arrangements for a similar conference we're holding there later on. In November.

Malone: Sorry, Mr Gräber. I didn't get where you are going …

Gräber: Lagos, L-a- … got it? Good. Now. Para. Jim told me that everyone taking part in the Canada conference will be writing a critique, and I want …

Malone: I'm sorry. Could you spell that for me?

Gräber: Critique? Yes. C-r-i-t-i-q-u-e. And I want Jim to collate these reports, and then we'll send copies to each company in the group, you see. I'll be sending him the circulation list.

Malone: I see. Erm, when will you send it? Shall I say …

Gräber: Oh, when I get round to it. You'll be reminding me, I expect. Now. The other thing. Yes, para. Thank him and his wife for their hospitality and so on. Yes? They looked after us very well.

Malone: Is there any particular thing you want me to mention?

Gräber: No. Erm, yes. We had a rather pleasant evening on the Friday, all together, with his family. We enjoyed that. Can you do something on those lines?

Malone: Oh, I think so. Anything else?

Gräber: Yes. They're probably coming to Switzerland in December. Around Christmas time; so, para. Then put something saying that I hope they will let us entertain them when they're here. Something like that, yes? And I'll just sign it Erich. OK?

Malone: Yes, Mr Gräber. I've got that. Erm, are you spending the whole morning with Mr Hoffman?

Gräber: I'll be with him for a couple of hours. Probably back here about twelve.

Malone: Fine. I'll have the letter ready for you to sign at twelve, then.

Gräber: Excellent. Thank you, Mary. Now, the next thing … *(Fade)*

Comprehension Questions

1. What sort of letter is it that Gräber is asking Mary to draft for him?
   A thanking letter.

2. Where has Gräber been?
   At a regional planning conference in Canada.

3. How does Gräber want the letter to start?

Introductory Recording

With a reference to him and his wife stopping off at Montreal, which Jim Harris said they should.

4   What was the next main point?
    The planning conference.

5   Is Gräber grateful to Jim for the part he played?
    Yes.

6   Are there going to be any more such conferences?
    Yes. Gräber is going to Lagos in November to make arrangements for a similar one.

7   Can you remember what Jim Harris is to do with the participants' reports on the Canadian conference?
    He is to collate them.

8   What did Gräber want the last paragraph to be about?
    He wanted to thank Harris and his wife for their hospitality, and to say that he hoped to return it when they come to Switzerland in December.

Text: The Thanking Letter

The words and phrases in italics are quoted verbatim from the Text.

Comprehension Questions

1   Who suggested going to Montreal?
    Mr Harris / Jim.

2   When did Erich and his wife go to Montreal?
    After the conference.

3   What did they think of Montreal?
    They thought it was *a fascinating city*.

4   How many conferences of this kind have Schweibur held before?
    None.

5   Was this one successful?
    Yes, it was.

6   Who contributed a good deal to this success?
    Mr Harris.

7   How valuable does Erich think the conference was for the participants?
    He is *convinced* it was of *great value*.

8   Does he hope to hold similar conferences in the future?
    Yes, he hopes they *will become regular practice throughout the group*.

9   Where is he going next month?
    To Lagos.

10 Why?
To make arrangements for a similar conference.

11 When will they be holding this conference?
They will be holding it *in November.*

12 What will each participant be doing?
They'll be *writing a critique of the conference.*

13 What does Erich want Harris to do with these critiques?
Collate them *into a report.*

14 Why?
So that they can *be circulated to other interested companies.*

15 What did Erich and his wife very much appreciate in Toronto?
The hospitality extended to them.

16 What does Erich particularly thank Jim for?
The pleasant evening they *spent* with him and his *family.*

17 When are the Harrises coming to Switzerland?
Sometime in December.

18 What does Erich hope the Harrises will do then?
He hopes they will let him *return* their *hospitality.*

Key to the Exercises

Exercise A
1 Due to his *efforts* the seminar was extremely successful.
2 We must *return* their hospitality.
3 There were twenty *participants* at the seminar.
4 Could you thank him for the hospitality he *extended* to us?
5 We *followed* his suggestion and stopped off at London.
6 I am *convinced* that the meeting will be valuable.
7 I certainly found it a *fascinating* city.
8 I hope to arrange similar conferences *throughout* our Group.
9 Drop a line to Jim saying how much we *appreciated* his hospitality, could you?
10 I spent a very pleasant evening with him and his family.

Exercise B

Miss Miller: What time *will* these visitors *be arriving*?

Mary Malone: I *will be picking* them *up* at the airport at eleven and *bringing* them here. They *will be* with Mr Gräber until lunch. They *will be visiting* the Training Department in the afternoon.

Miss Miller: Well, Mr Konstanz *won't be* very pleased. He *will be* tied up all next week, you know.

Key to the Exercises

Mary Malone: I think Mr Gräber *will be calling* a meeting about it fairly soon. But don't worry, there *won't be* much to discuss, so it *won't take* very long.

Miss Miller: Oh, good. I hope Mr Konstanz can make it. And how long are these people staying here?

Mary Malone: Oh, they *will* only *be* here for one day. They *will be leaving* the next morning.

Exercise C

1. I shall take my holiday *at* Easter.
2. Schweibur was founded *in* 1924.
3. Mary doesn't like going out by herself *at* night.
4. 'And for heaven's sake be *on* time for a change.'
5. We got there *in* plenty of time.
6. I hope there'll be some snow *at* Christmas.
7. Mr Gräber will be back *on* the morning of 23rd.
8. The factory closes down for a month *in* summer.
9. I'm hoping to get away for a bit *in* April.
10. Mr Boileau is leaving *on* the afternoon of 4th.

Language Laboratory Part 1: Tapescript

Drill 1

Ann Miller is secretary to Schweibur's Training Manager, Mr Konstanz. When someone rings up to make an appointment to see Mr Konstanz, she consults his diary.

1. (Example) I wonder if I could see Mr Konstanz for about an hour on Monday morning?
Mr Konstanz is attending a seminar at nine o'clock, I'm afraid, but he'll be free in the afternoon.

2. (Example) Well, what about Tuesday afternoon?
Mr Konstanz is briefing the training staff at half past two, I'm afraid, but he'll be free in the morning.

3. No, it'll have to be Thursday morning, then.
Mr Konstanz is holding a committee meeting at half past ten, I'm afraid, but he'll be free in the afternoon.

4. I'm tied up in the afternoon. But I could make Friday, say about half past three.
Mr Konstanz is showing visitors round at three o'clock, I'm afraid, but he'll be free in the morning.

5. Oh, dear, then it'll have to be the week after. How about Monday morning?
Mr Konstanz is inspecting a new training area at half past nine, I'm afraid, but he'll be free in the afternoon.

6   No, I'm afraid I'm busy then until Wednesday afternoon.
    Mr Konstanz is speaking at a management conference at two o'clock, I'm afraid, but he'll be free in the morning.

7   Well, can I invite him to have lunch with me on Thursday?
    Mr Konstanz is having lunch with Mr Engren at one o'clock, I'm afraid, but he'll be free in the afternoon.

8   Friday afternoon is the only other time I'm free.
    Mr Konstanz is flying to Denmark at half past two, I'm afraid, but he'll be free in the morning.

    Oh, dear, then I won't be able to see him at all.

Drill 2

Ann Miller is reminding her boss of the times people are coming to see him during the coming week.

1   (Example)   When's Johnson coming?
    Mr Johnson's coming at ten o'clock in the morning, on Wednesday 27th.

2   (Example)   Can you just remind me when Duclos is turning up?
    Mr Duclos is coming at three o'clock in the afternoon, on Monday 25th.

3   I forget when Heine is coming.
    Mr Heine is coming at nine o'clock in the morning, on Friday 29th.

4   Is it on Tuesday that I'm seeing Milewski?
    Mr Milewski is coming at two thirty in the afternoon, on Thursday 28th.

5   I can't quite remember when that man Dupont is turning up.
    Mr Dupont is coming at eleven in the morning, on Monday 25th.

6   And when's Pellegrini due?
    Mr Pellegrini is coming at four o'clock in the afternoon, On Thursday 28th.

7   When is Steiner meeting me for dinner?
    Mr Steiner is coming at seven o'clock in the evening, on Saturday 30th.

8   Is it this week that Nilsson arrives?
    Mr Nilsson is coming at two o'clock in the afternoon, on Friday 29th.

Pronunciation Practice

In this unit we're going to study three English vowel sounds. Listen to the example words that are given in your book.

1   *lark*

2   *lock*

3   *luck*

Can you heat the difference between them? Which one is this?
lock

That was number two. Did you get that right? Now, which one is this?
luck

Language Laboratory Part 1

That was number three. And which one is this?
lock

That was number two again. And now this one?
lark

Yes, that one was easy. It was number one. Now we're going to say ten words. You must decide whether the sound is like example one, two or three, and write the number down. Are you ready? Listen carefully.

1	*dock*		6	*darn*
2	*hum*		7	*suck*
3	*carp*		8	*much*
4	*stock*		9	*shark*
5	*cot*		10	*boss*

Now here are the correct answers:
One was number two   Six was number one
Two was number three   Seven was number three
Three was number one   Eight was number three
Four was number two   Nine was number one
Five was number two   Ten was number two

How many of these did you get right? Now let's practise the pronunciation of these three sounds. Look at the limerick in your book. Listen to it first.

Said the boss to Miss Martin your job is
To reply to our customer Dobbies.
This draft's rather rough
But I trust it's enough;
Send the top and keep two carbon copies.

Now repeat the limerick line by line, paying attention to the example vowel sounds and to the length of the syllables printed in capitals.

Dialogue

Someone rings Mr Karlberger's office to make an appointment. Mrs Lindfors answers the telephone.

Kraus: Hello, is that Karlberger's office?

Mrs Lindfors: Yes, it is. Can I help you?

Kraus: I'd like to make an appointment to see Mr Karlberger.

Mrs Lindfors: Who's speaking, please?

Kraus: My name is Kraus. Mr Karlberger asked me to contact him and arrange a meeting.

Mrs Lindfors: I see. When would be a convenient time for you, Mr Kraus?

Kraus: Tuesday of next week would be best from my point of view.

Mrs Lindfors: I'm afraid Mr Karlberger has appointments for the whole of Tuesday. Would Monday be convenient?

Kraus: Well, I can't make Monday afternoon, so it'll have to be the morning, if that's OK.

Mrs Lindfors: Yes, would any particular time suit you?

Kraus: I'd like to make it fairly early if possible.

Mrs Lindfors: Shall we say nine o'clock, then?

Kraus: Fine. Thank you very much.

Mrs Lindfors: We look forward to seeing you then, Mr Kraus. Goodbye and thank you for calling.

Correspondence

In this Key suggestions for an acceptable version are printed in bold type.

Dear John,

After the conference we **followed your suggestion** of going round some of the colleges, which we **thoroughly** enjoyed. This was the first time we had been to England, **a wonderful experience we shall long remember. Thank you so very much for looking after us and making our stay so interesting.**

The conference in Amsterdam **is/will be** from 12th to 14th November. I think **we will probably meet/we will probably be meeting** in the International Training Centre at 9.30 am **on** the Monday, when Mr A L Walgrave of the Management Institute, Chicago, **will address** us. I understand he **will be speaking** on 'Recent Developments in Management Training'. **I will send** you a conference programme when this is fully worked out. I **am working** on it next week.

Yours,

Telegrams

The conference has finished early, and I will be back tomorrow.

We confirm that we have reserved a single room with shower for three days from 28th of the month.

1   ACKNOWLEDGE RECEIPT ORDER THREE FOUR FIVE TWO STOP LETTER FOLLOWS

2 PERRIER IN HOSPITAL DUE ACCIDENT STOP MALAFOSSE ARRIVING YOUR OFFICE NINE TOMORROW STOP PLEASE CONFIRM OK

Language Laboratory Part 2: Tapescript

Drill 3

Mrs Lindfors often receives telephone calls from people wishing to meet her boss, Mr Karlberger. Sometimes they ask to see him at times that are just not convenient. When this happens, Mrs Lindfors passes on their request to Mr Karlberger, who tells her when he can see the caller. Unfortunately, Mr Karlberger isn't always very polite on such occasions and Mrs Lindfors has to re-phrase what he says when she speaks to the caller.

1 (Example) What, Steiner again? Well, I'm engaged this afternoon. Tell him ten tomorrow morning.
I'm afraid Mr Karlberger is engaged this afternoon, Mr Steiner. Would tomorrow morning at ten be convenient?

2 (Example) What on earth does Gräber want now? Well, I'm busy at the moment—make it three this afternoon.
I'm afraid Mr Karlberger is busy at the moment, Mr Gräber. Would this afternoon at three be convenient?

3 Duclos? I'm in a meeting, damn it. Nine o'clock Friday is the earliest I can see him.
I'm afraid Mr Karlberger is in a meeting, Mr Duclos. Would Friday at nine o'clock be convenient?

4 I'm away tomorrow. Tell Mrs Sanchez Wednesday afternoon at four.
I'm afraid Mr Karlberger is away tomorrow, Mrs Sanchez. Would Wednesday afternoon at four be convenient?

5 But I saw Koster only yesterday! And you know I'm in conference this morning. Oh well, tell him to be here at ten tomorrow.
I'm afraid Mr Karlberger is in conference, Mr Koster. Would tomorrow at ten be convenient?

6 Tell the good Mr White that I'm leaving for Germany tomorrow, and that if he wants to see me he'd better come this afternoon at five.
I'm afraid Mr Karlberger is leaving for Germany tomorrow, Mr White. Would this afternoon at five be convenient?

Drill 4

Ann Miller is very helpful. If a visitor to the company is in difficulty she always offers her assistance.

1 (Example) I'm having a bit of difficulty booking hotel rooms for my trip.
Perhaps I can help you. Shall I book them for you?

2 (Example) I don't see how I'm going to find time to look for a present for my wife.
Perhaps I can help you. Shall I look for one for you?

3 I've been trying to find that report for half an hour.
Perhaps I can help you. Shall I try to find it for you?

4 Oh, dear, I'm sure I'm going to be late for my next appointment. I wonder if I could ring up Grunbass.
Perhaps I can help you. Shall I ring them up for you?

5 The trouble is, I haven't got a timetable to look up when the next train leaves.
Perhaps I can help you. Shall I look it up for you?

6 Oh, dear, I'll have to fetch my briefcase from the other building—where Mr Karlberger's office is.
Perhaps I can help you. Shall I fetch it for you?

7 I have terrible difficulty translating these forms into English.
Perhaps I can help you. Shall I translate them for you?

8 I'm afraid there are rather a lot of mistakes in this letter. Unfortunately my English isn't very good, so it'll need correcting.
Perhaps I can help you. Shall I correct it for you?

Active Listening

Passage 1: Listen to this short telephone conversation. Erich Gräber is ringing Anna Mackenzie.

Erich: Anna, is that you?

Anna: Erich, how are you?

Erich: Fine, fine. Look, could you tell Jim my damn plane's been held up by a strike, and may be anything up to three hours late at your airport. I may well not make it this afternoon, but if it's OK with him, I'll ring him from my hotel when I finally get there, and fix a time to see him tomorrow? OK?

Anna: Yes, fine. I'll let him know when he's back from lunch.

Erich: Thanks very much. 'Bye.

Anna: 'Bye.

1 What has delayed Gräber's plane?
A strike.

2 How late will it be?
Anything up to three hours.

3 Will Gräber arrive this afternoon?
He *may well not*.

4   What will Gräber do when he gets to his hotel?
    He'll *ring him. (Jim)*

5   Why?
    To *fix a time to see him tomorrow.*

6   Now write down the message Anna should give Jim.
    Erich's plane has been delayed. He may not arrive this afternoon. He will phone from his hotel when he arrives, to arrange a time to see you tomorrow.

Passage 2: Mary Malone received this telephone call the other day.

Daly: Could I have a word with Mr Gräber, please. It's Daly from Schweibur Dublin speaking.

Mary Malone: I'm afraid Mr Gräber is at lunch. Can I ask him to ring you back?

Daly: Well, perhaps you could just give him a message. Could you tell him that because of a rail strike next week I'm sending a car to Dublin Airport to pick him up next Tuesday? The man will be wearing a Schweibur uniform, and will wait for Mr Gräber just the other side of customs. OK?

Mary Malone: Thank you very much, Mr Daly. I'll tell Mr Gräber when he gets back from lunch.

Daly: Thank you so much. Goodbye.

Mary Malone: Goodbye, and thank you.

What is the message Mary should give to Mr Gräber?
Mr Daly is sending a car to meet you at Dublin Airport as there is a rail strike. The man will wait the other side of customs and will be wearing a Schweibur uniform.

Passage 3: Your boss isn't in this morning. But he recorded a message on the dictaphone.

In my in-tray you'll find an invitation to a dinner party from Mr Karlberger. Could you drop a line to the effect that I'll be unable to attend, the usual thing.

What have you to do?
Reply to the invitation. Thank Mr Karlberger for his kind invitation, but say that your boss regrets he is unable to accept (as he has a previous engagement).

Role Simulation

Situation

In this unit the students are asked to imagine that an employee from one of their company's overseas branches is attending a six-week training course at their company. Their boss has asked them to help the visitor by answering all his questions about life in their country and procedures within their company.

Procedure

In this Role Simulation the teacher should play the part of the visitor throughout. Guidelines on the topics are given below, but during the secretary's explanation the teacher/visitor should query any point that isn't clear and should add questions of his own.

Teacher's Roles

1 I understand that I have . . . *(time)* for lunch. What do most people do about food in the middle of the day? Is there a canteen or anything?

2 Look, I can't speak the language very well. I really need to have some kind of language course to help me improve it. Where should I go?

3 But suppose I fall ill while I'm here. Is there a health service? What would I do?

4 I think the best way of getting to know people here would be to join a club of some sort. I'm keen on sport. What facilities are available?

5 Look, the company have put me in a hotel for six weeks. I don't much like hotel life. Is there any alternative accommodation I could get? Would it be possible to rent a flat for such a short time?

6 Suppose I want to send a memo to someone in the company here. What's the procedure for internal post?

7 I haven't got my car here, so I'll have to rely on public transport. I'd be grateful if you could tell me about the different ways of travelling. Can you get season tickets?

8 I've already spent quite a lot of my own money on company business and I would like to reclaim my expenses. How should I do this?

9 Look, could you explain about the banks here? How do I open an account?

10 Would you mind explaining all about the telephones here? What happens when I want to make an internal call, for example, or when I want a foreign call?

Key to 'What is this'

Page 32: briefcase
Page 33: in- and out-trays
Page 40: pencil and ruler

Unit 4

Unit Summary

Introductory Recording	This episode is entitled 'A Message fom Copenhagen'. Mary Malone receives a telephone call from Schweibur's associate company in Copenhagen and has to take a message for her boss, Mr Gräber.
Text	The Text is the written form of the message Mary Malone received.
Vocabulary	There is a two-part exercise which deals with the vocabulary of telephoning.
Structures	1 Clauses of purpose (Exercise B and Drill 2) expressed by the use of a simple infinitive b *so as (not)* + infinitive c *so that* 2 Phrasal verbs with *put* (Exercise C and Drill 1)
Pronunciation Practice	This deals with the difference between the vowel sounds [o] as in *cot*, [ɔ] as in *caught* and [əʊ] as in *coat*. There is an ear-training exercise followed by repetition of a limerick.
Dialogue	The situation is that of a customer cancelling an appointment.
Correspondence	There is a draft letter to be corrected.
Telegrams	There are four telegrams, two to be decoded and two to be encoded.
Gambits	Drill 3: Asking for repetition. *I'm so sorry, but I didn't quite catch what you said after . . .* Drill 4: Accepting invitations on behalf of the boss. *I'm sure Mr Schulz would be delighted to . . . , Mr . . . . I'll ask him to . . . .*
Active Listening	There are two passages in this unit. 1 A telephone message. The student has to answer comprehension questions. 2 A dictated letter. The student is not required to take down the whole dictation, but has to answer questions of the type: *What were the last two words you heard?*
Role Simulation	The students are asked to imagine that their boss is ill and that they have to deal with visitors who come to the office to see him. There are roles

for the student. The teacher is required to play the part of the visitor throughout.

Homework

The written gambits introduced in this unit deal with:

Making suggestions and proposals
Asking for approval
Confirmation

Introductory Recording

Tapescript

A Message from Copenhagen

Mary Malone is personal secretary to Erich Gräber, Assistant Marketing Manager of Schweibur International. Mr Gräber is in Lagos, and Mary is running the office in his absence. This afternoon there is a call from Andersen's, Schweibur's associate company in Copenhagen.

Malone: Mr Gräber's office. Good afternoon.

Receptionist: There's a call from Andersen's Copenhagen. A Mr Jensen.

Malone: Put it through, please.

Receptionist: You're through now, Mr Jensen.

Jensen: Thank you, thank you. Hello? Arne Jensen here.

Malone: Good afternoon, Mr Jensen.

Jensen: Good afternoon. Well, now, that must be the nice Miss Malone.

Malone: Yes, that's right. This is Mary Malone. How are you, Mr Jensen?

Jensen: Oh, I'm all right. Carrying on as ever. Getting a bit older every day. And you?

Malone: I'm fine, thank you.

Jensen: Good, good. It was very pleasant to see you at the fiftieth anniversary the month before last.

Malone: It was nice you were able to get down for it.

Jensen: You really mean that, Mary?

Malone: Mr Jensen. Now, how can I help you?

Jensen: Well, if we can't put it off any longer. Is your nice boss in?

Malone: No, I'm sorry, he's away on a trip. Can I, er . . .

Jensen: Oh, that is a pity. Always running around, isn't he? When's he back? Fairly soon?

Malone: I'm sorry, I can't tell you exactly. He's gone to Lagos, to set up a

Introductory Recording

regional conference. And he's staying longer than we expected. I'm sorry. It's rather unusual.

Jensen: So you're all by yourself? Perhaps you need someone to talk to.

Malone: There are quite a few other people in this building, actually, Mr Jensen.

Jensen: Well, I wish I was.

Malone: Now, Mr Jensen, I'm quite sure you didn't ring me up just so as to say things like that to me. Now, what can I do for you?

Jensen: Yes, you're right. To business. It's about the new switchboard we're producing here. The one we're calling the Fonomat. Have you heard about it?

Malone: I think I put the file away just the other day. Can you hold on a moment, so that I can get it? Hold on, please.

Malone: Mr Jensen? Fonomat SBA 73. Is that it?

Jensen: That's it. You are efficient. Well, now. There are three fairly important questions I want to put down for Mr Gräber. Ready?

Malone: Yes.

Jensen: Oh, and I think Mr Gräber's coming to Copenhagen next week, isn't he? So that we'll get our answers from him then. Now. First of all, what type of publicity is he thinking of putting out? Does he want any special photographs? You know, of any of the Fonomat mechanisms, that sort of thing. Or technical drawings instead. Anything that . . .

Malone: I'm so sorry, Mr Jensen. I didn't quite catch what you said after mechanism.

Jensen: What? Oh technical drawings. Does he want any prepared . . .

Malone: . . . or technical drawings for publicity material? Yes. Got that.

Jensen: Second. Packaging. Any special ideas? This is quite important. We have to put in for the packaging materials at a fairly early stage. So that we're not short of anything when the first Fonomat units come off the assembly line. That would put everything back. Delivery dates and so on. And there's a great shortage of these materials, as you know. So, if there are any special instructions . . .

Malone: Right, Mr Jensen. I've got that. And the third thing?

Jensen: Yes, the last thing is sales orders. Some distributors, especially in Africa and South America, are putting in much bigger initial orders than we expected. So that we won't be able to meet them at once. Now, if . . .

Malone: Sorry, Mr Jensen. I didn't follow that. Could you . . .

Jensen: Sorry, my fault. Let's take an example. We were expecting orders for 320 units each from Lagos and Caracas. So this is what we are producing for them at the moment. But now the actual orders have arrived and they've put in for 400 each. So that the question is, do we give Lagos 400 and Caracas only 240 now, with 160 later on? Or is there another way round it? Do you see the . . .

Malone: Oh, yes, I've got it now. Right, Mr Jensen, I'll see Mr Gräber gets the message.

Jensen: Yes, we must arrange things so as not to put anyone out, mustn't we? Fine. Thank you, nice Mary. And tell Gräber I'll put him up when he comes up here, if he'd like that.

Malone: I'm sure he'd be delighted to stay with you, Mr Jensen. So. Goodbye for now.

Jensen: Goodbye, Mary. And thank you. See you again soon, I hope.

Malone: Thank you, Mr Jensen. Goodbye.

Comprehension Questions

1. Who rang Mr Gräber's office?
   Mr Jensen (from Andersen's in Copenhagen).

2. Why couldn't Mr Jensen speak to Mr Gräber?
   Because he was away on a trip (to Lagos).

3. What is Mr Jensen's attitude to Mary Malone?
   He likes her (and tries to flirt with her).

4. Can you remember which product Mr Jensen was phoning about?
   The new switchboard they're producing in Copenhagen (called the Fonomat).

5. What does Mr Jensen want Mary to do?
   To take down three important questions for Mr Gräber to answer.

6. What was the first question about?
   About the type of publicity. (Should they get special photographs or technical drawings?)

7. What was the second question about?
   Packaging.

8. Why is it important to reach a decision on packaging soon?
   There's a shortage of materials and they must order early (so as not to hold things up).

9. What is the third problem?
   Some distributors are putting in bigger orders than they expected. (How are they going to decide on quotas?)

10. What does Mr Jensen offer to do?
    To put Mr Gräber up when he comes to Copenhagen (next week).

Introductory Recording

Text: A Telephone Message

Comprehension Questions

The words and phrases in italics are quoted verbatim from the Text.

1. When was the message received?
   At *10.45 am* on *5th August*.

2. What did Mr Jensen phone about?
   He *rang up about the new Fonomat switchboard Andersen's is currently producing*.

3. Why does he want Mr Gräber to give his attention to the three points in the message?
   So that they *can come to some decision* when Mr Gräber meets him *in Copenhagen next week*.

4. What decision must they come to about the publicity material they're going to put out?
   They must decide *whether to include special photographs or technical drawings to illustrate the mechanisms of the Fonomat*.

5. What is the second thing Mr Jensen wants to know?
   He wants to know if Mr Gräber has *any special ideas on packaging*.

6. Why does Mr Jensen consider it essential to put in for packaging materials now?
   So that they won't be short of anything when the first units come off the assembly line.

7. What is the problem regarding orders of packaging materials?
   These materials are in short supply and delivery times are most unreliable.

8. What does Mr Jensen want to avoid?
   He's anxious to avoid any hold-ups.

9. What is the problem regarding sales orders?
   Some regional distributors are putting in much bigger orders than anticipated.

10. How many units did they originally think Lagos and Caracas would order?
    They thought they would order *320 units each*.

11. As a result, what did they do?
    They fixed their production schedule accordingly.

12. What has now happened?
    These branches have put in for 400 units each.

13. What does Mr Jensen want advice on?
    He wants advice on *how best to allocate his limited supply*.

14. What does he not want to do?
    He doesn't want to *upset any of the distributors*.

15 What did Mr Jensen offer to do?
He offered *to put Mr Gräber up next week*.

16 What does Mary Malone want to know?
She wants to know if she should *write and confirm Mr Gräber's acceptance*.

Key to the Exercises

Exercise A

1 Very often you can *dial* a call direct.
2 But sometimes you have to go through the *operator*.
3 Outside calls sometimes go through the *switchboard*.
4 Each telephone within the company has its own *extension* number.
5 The numbers of most *subscribers* can be found in the telephone *directory*.
6 Calls within the same area are known as *local* calls.
7 Long-distance calls are known as *trunk* calls.
8 Usually calls between people in the same building are called *internal* calls.
9 If an outside call is put through to the wrong office it has to be *transferred*.
10 When the person receiving the call pays for it, the call is known as a *reverse* charge call.

Joan Wright: What do I do if I want to *ring* somebody *up*?

Mary Malone: Well, if it's somebody in the company you can *look up* the number on this list here, then simply dial the number. For outside calls, you dial nine before the number. Of course, if you can't *get through* you have to try again later.

Joan Wright: What about incoming calls for people on other extensions?

Mary Malone: If you want to *put* a call *through* to somebody else, you press this button and then dial the number. Then just *put* your receiver *down* again when somebody *picks* the phone *up*. But wait until they **do** answer or you'll *cut* the caller *off*.

Joan Wright: And if the number is engaged?

Mary Malone: If it's engaged, you press the button again to speak to the caller, and ask him to *hold on* for a few moments or *ring back* later.

Joan Wright: And if the person is out, I suppose I take a message?

Mary Malone: Yes, you *take* it *down* on one of these special pads. And you mustn't forget to *find out/take down* the caller's name and telephone number.

Exercise B

1 Would you mind putting these documents in the horizontal file so as not to crease them?
2 Would you mind signing the petty cash slips so that I can do the accounts today?

Key to the Exercises

3 Would you mind phoning Mr Schulz to cancel your game of golf at the weekend?
4 Would you mind checking the new filing system so that I can type out the index?
5 Would you mind getting home before six tonight to help your wife with the party arrangements?
6 Would you mind trying to be on time for the meeting this afternoon so as not to upset Mr Boileau?
7 Would you mind arranging for a car to meet Mr Costello to take him to his hotel?
8 Would you mind returning Mr Gräber's passport so that he can renew it?
9 Would you mind settling Invoice Number 41036 so as not to cause any further unpleasantness?
10 Would you mind circulating the quarterly statement so that the Management Committee can see it before the next meeting?

Exercise C

Not all the possible tenses have been indicated in this Key.

1 Mr Gräber offered to put him up.
2 Would you mind putting it away in my drawer?
3 They have just put up a new building.
4 The secretary was put out by his rude remarks.
5 Don't forget to put it back in the files.
6 We won't put up with it any longer.
7 I'll put you through to him.
8 The branches have put in for 400 units each.
9 We were put off by the weather.
10 He told me to put it down on paper.
11 Don't put it off till tomorrow.
12 I think we should put it forward at the next meeting.

Language Laboratory Part 1: Tapescript

Drill 1

Miss Miller and Mrs Lindfors are talking to each other in the office.

1 (Example) I couldn't get a hotel for the Frenchman. Did Mr Konstanz take him home?
I suppose he must have put him up.

2 (Example) Have you heard that Jutta's moving to Accounts? I wonder if she actually applied for that transfer?
I suppose she must have put in for it.

3 Nobody's turned up for the meeting. I wonder if they cancelled it.
I suppose they must have put it off.

4   That file that was on your desk—did you replace it?
    I suppose I must have put it back.

5   I hear Ilse's left. I'm surprised she's stuck it so long. I know I couldn't stand working in that office.
    I suppose she must have put up with it.

6   Is Mr Konstanz still waiting for his call, or did the operator deal with it?
    I suppose she must have put him through.

7   I'm looking for that letter that was on your desk—but you've tidied everything.
    I suppose I must have put it away.

8   Take a look at this invoice. Aren't their prices rather high, or has there been another increase?
    I suppose they must have put them up.

9   I think Mr Konstanz was rather angry about the remarks that were passed.
    I suppose he must have been put out by them.

Drill 2

Miss Walter from the Personnel Department is asking Miss Miller about her work.

1   (Example)   Mr Konstanz is reorganizing the filing system, isn't he?
    Yes, he's reorganizing the filing system to make it more efficient.

2   (Example)   And do you sort the documents before filing?
    Yes, we sort the documents before filing so as not to waste time.

3   (Example)   You keep the files in this office, I suppose?
    Yes, we keep the files in this office so that Mr Konstanz has access to them.

4   And do you order stationery in good time?
    Yes, we always order stationery in good time to make sure we don't run out.

5   You make a note of what you need, do you?
    Yes, we make a note of what we need so as not to forget it.

6   And you sort the mail every morning, of course.
    Yes, we sort the mail every morning so that it's ready for Mr Konstanz.

7   Do you put large plans in the horizontal file?
    Yes, we put large plans in the horizontal file so as not to crease them.

8   And you deal with incoming calls?
    Yes, we deal with incoming calls so that Mr Konstanz isn't bothered.

9   And you're retyping the filing index, I see.
    Yes, we're retyping the filing index to bring it up to date.

Language Laboratory Part 1

Pronunciation Practice

In this unit we're going to study three rather difficult vowel sounds. Listen to the three examples that are given in your book.

1 *cot*

2 *caught*

3 *coat*

Can you hear the difference between them? Which one is this?
cot

That was number one. Which one is this?
coat

That was number three. Now which one is this?
cot

That was number one again. Now listen carefully to numbers one and two together.
cot
caught

Do you hear the difference between those two? Which one is this?
caught

Yes, that was number two. Now listen to numbers two and three together.
caught
coat

Which one is this?
caught

That was number two again. Now we're going to say ten words. Decide whether the vowel sound is like example one, two or three, and write the number down. Are you ready? Listen carefully.

1	*code*	6	*cope*
2	*born*	7	*gauze*
3	*cork*	8	*fox*
4	*tot*	9	*rod*
5	*poke*	10	*porch*

Now here are the correct answers.

One was number three   Six was number three
Two was number two   Seven was number two
Three was number two   Eight was number one
Four was number one   Nine was number one
Five was number three   Ten was number two

Now we're going to have another limerick to practise these three vowels. Look at your book and listen first.

'I loathe filing', said Joan, 'it's a bore.
Like tidying up, it's a chore.
I must start, I suppose,
'Cos these drawers just won't close,
And reports lie all over the floor.'

Now repeat the limerick line by line, paying attention to the example vowel sounds and to the long loud syllables printed in capital letters.

Dialogue

Mr Heine is out of his office in the sales section when an important potential customer telephones to cancel an appointment. His secretary, Betty Wood, has to deal with the situation.

McAlister: Hello, is that Mr Heine's office?

Wood: Yes, it is.

McAlister: Is Heine in?

Wood: No, I'm afraid he isn't. This is his secretary speaking, can I help you?

McAlister: I should think so, yes. This is McAlister, from Robertsons Ltd, Toronto. I wonder if you could tell Heine that I shan't be coming to Zurich next week after all, and so won't be able to meet him.

Wood: Oh, that's a pity, Mr McAlister. I know Mr Heine was very much looking forward to meeting you.

McAlister: Well, I'm afraid there are personal reasons that make it impossible for me to come next week.

Wood: Oh, I see.

McAlister: But you can tell Heine that I shall be in touch, probably in about two weeks' time.

Wood: Oh good. He'll be glad to hear that.

McAlister: Right, that's all for the moment then.

Wood: Well, we look forward to hearing from you, Mr McAlister.

McAlister: Oh, you will. Goodbye.

Wood: Goodbye, and thank you for calling.

Correspondence

In this Key suggestions for an acceptable version are printed in bold type.

Dear Mr Akwekwe,

Thank you for your letter **of** 12th July **in which you order** 400 Fonomat switchboards *(omit)*.

It is rather unfortunate that you **have now decided** to change your original **order**. The allocation you initially put **in for** was only 320 units. We cannot alter our **production** schedule **to increase** your quota **at** the moment. However, we are **extremely / very** pleased that you think there will be **a good market** for the Fonomat and we **will do** everything we can **to** supply you with 400 units.

(omit) To do this we **will have** to send *(omit)* you your allocation in two **instalments**. You **will receive** 250 units **at** the beginning of this month and the **remainder** by the beginning of August. I hope this won't be putting **you out**.

I would be **most** *(or omit)* grateful if you can estimate how **many** units you will need in the last quarter of 1977 **so that we can increase** your next quota.

Yours sincerely,

Telegrams

Our order which was due to be delivered on the fifth of this month has not arrived. Please attend to this matter urgently.

We urgently need product number 507. We want to order 500 of these.

1. OFFER UNACCEPTABLE CHAIRMAN STOP AWAIT INSTRUCTIONS STOP

2. ORDER SB STROKE FOUR FOUR TWO UNCLEARED CUSTOMS STOP SEND COPY EXPORT DOCUMENT THREE ONE TWO SOONEST

Language Laboratory Part 2: Tapescript

Drill 3

When Mr Gräber is out of the office, his secretary, Miss Malone, takes messages for him over the telephone. Often, however, the line is rather bad and she has to ask the caller to repeat part of what they have said.

1. (Example) Could you tell Mr Gräber that, although I accept his first point, I'm . . .
I'm so sorry, but I didn't quite catch what you said after 'accept his first point'.

2. (Example) And could you tell him that we thank him for his offer, but that . . .
I'm so sorry, but I didn't quite catch what you said after 'thank him for his offer'.

3. I shall be staying at the Continental Hotel, and look . . .
I'm so sorry, but I didn't quite catch what you said after 'staying at the Continental Hotel'.

4. There'll be three of us coming next week, and we hope . . .
I'm so sorry, but I didn't quite catch what you said after 'coming next week'.

5. Now, could you put the following item on the agenda; the committee . . .
I'm so sorry, but I didn't quite catch what you said after 'committee'.

6. Well, in the end it turned out that their main objections were, firstly that they . . .
I'm so sorry, but I didn't quite catch what you said after 'their main objections'.

7. Could you let him know that I'm seeing Braun tomorrow, and that . . .
I'm so sorry, but I didn't quite catch what you said after 'seeing Braun tomorrow'.

8. At Gräber's request, I'm leaving for Paris next week, but I don't . . .
I'm so sorry, but I didn't quite catch what you said after 'leaving for Paris next week'.

Drill 4

Schweibur's Personnel Manager, Mr Schulz, is often taken out for a meal or a drink by his colleagues. He is often out of the office when people ring him up, so his secretary, Mrs Pau, accepts the invitations on his behalf.

1. (Example) Hoffman here. Would Schulz care to join me for lunch, do you think?
I'm sure Mr Schulz would be delighted to join you for lunch, Mr Hoffman.

2. (Example) Steiner speaking. Post and I were wondering if Schulz would fancy having a drink with us about twelvish?
I'm sure Mr Schulz would be delighted to have a drink with you, Mr Steiner.

3. This is Maier speaking. It's such a lovely day I thought Mr Schulz might like to fit in a round of golf after work.
I'm sure Mr Schulz would be delighted to fit in a round of golf, Mr Maier.

4   Borg here. I was wondering if Schulz would like to have dinner with my wife and me on Wednesday.
    I'm sure Mr Schulz would be delighted to have dinner with you and you wife, Mr Borg.

Although Mrs Pau is confident that Mr Schulz will accept the invitation, she also tells the caller that he will confirm his acceptance.

1   (Example)   Hoffman here. Would Schulz care to join me for lunch, do you think?
    I'm sure Mr Schulz would be delighted to join you for lunch, Mr Hoffman. I'll ask him to ring you when he gets in.

2   (Example)   Steiner speaking. Post and I were wondering if Schulz would fancy having a drink with us about twelvish?
    I'm sure Mr Schulz would be delighted to have a drink with you, Mr Steiner. I'll ask him to let you know when he gets in.

3   This is Maier speaking. It's such a lovely day I thought Mr Schulz might like to fit in a round of golf after work.
    I'm sure Mr Schulz would be delighted to fit in a round of golf, Mr Maier. I'll ask him to give you a ring when he gets in.

4   Borg here. I was wondering if Schulz would like to have dinner with my wife and me on Wednesday.
    I'm sure Mr Schulz would be delighted to have dinner with you and your wife, Mr Borg. I'll ask him to confirm that when he gets in.

5   Müller speaking. There'll be a glass of sherry for Mr Schulz in the Board Room at about eleven if he'd like to come along.
    I'm sure he'd be delighted to come along, Mr Müller. I'll ask him to join you when he gets in.

6   Bruns here. I've got Gunarsson from Johannesson AB here tomorrow. Perhaps Mr Schulz would like to have lunch with us.
    I'm sure Mr Schulz would be delighted to have lunch with you, Mr Bruns. I'll ask him to let you know definitely when he gets in.

7   Flügel. One or two of us are thinking of trying the new Italian restaurant one day this week. Schulz care to join us?
    I'm sure Mr Schulz would be delighted to join you, Mr Flügel. I'll ask him to call you when he gets in.

8   Anders speaking. I'd like to invite Mr Schulz to be my guest tomorrow evening at Le Bistro.
    I'm sure Mr Schulz would be delighted to be your guest, Mr Anders. I'll ask him to confirm that when he gets in.

Active Listening

Passage 1: Mrs Lindfors' boss, Mr Karlberger, was away in Holland when Mr Wells rang from London.

Wells: Is that Karlberger's office?

Lindfors: Yes, it is, can I help you?

Wells: Well, this is Wells here. I know Mr Karlberger's in Rotterdam at the moment, but I was wondering if you could get a message to him.

Lindfors: Yes, certainly.

Wells: I made arrangements to meet him in Eindhoven tomorrow morning, but something's come up, and I don't think I'll be able to make it myself. If I don't, I'll be sending a Mr Carington in my place. Carington's my Purchasing Manager, knows all about it, and has my authority to discuss the whole question. Could you make a point of apologizing to Mr Karlberger for this inconvenience, and tell him that I'll be writing myself tomorrow if I don't get to Eindhoven.

Lindfors: Yes, I'll tell him that, Mr Wells. Thank you very much for calling.

Wells: Thank you so much. Goodbye.

Lindfors: Goodbye.

1. Who is calling?
   Mr Wells.

2. Will he definitely not be able to meet Mr Karlberger?
   No, but he probably won't be able to.

3. Who will take his place?
   Mr Carington.

4. Who is he?
   The Purchasing Manager.

5. How much authority will he have?
   He has Mr Wells' *authority to discuss the whole question.*

6. What else does the caller ask Mrs Lindfors to do?
   Apologize to Mr Karlberger for the inconvenience, and tell him that he'll be writing if he doesn't get to Eindhoven.

7. Now write down the message Mrs Lindfors should give to her boss.
   Mr Wells phoned to say he probably won't be able to meet you in Eindhoven tomorrow. Mr Carington, the Purchasing Manager, will take his place and has authority to discuss the whole question. Mr Wells apologizes for the inconvenience and will write if he can't meet you.

Passage 2: Mr Heine in the Sales Section has dictated a letter onto the dictaphone.

Language Laboratory Part 2

Dear Sirs,

With effect from the first of next month the prices of our BEX range are to be raised by 6%. Para.

We very much regret having to make this increase. It is unfortunately unavoidable in view of the rising cost of labour and raw materials in Sweden, and recent increases in taxation. Our view, however, is that even with this increase our prices remain highly competitive in a market which has seen many such price increases over the past two years. Para.

New price lists are currently being prepared, and will be forwarded to you as soon as they are available. So as not to adversely affect any business currently under negotiation, we will charge you at the old price for all orders received on or before May 15th.

Yours sincerely . . . . And that's for my signature.

1 What were the last four words you heard?
from the first of

2 What were the last four words you heard?
to be raised by

3 What are you to do with the last three words you heard?
Begin a new paragraph.

4 What were the last three words you heard?
in view of

5 What were the last two words you heard?
our view

6 What were the last four words that you heard?
even with this increase

7 What were the last two words you heard?
remain highly

8 What were the last four words you heard?
market which has seen

9 What were the last four words you heard?
so as not to

10 What were the last three words you heard?
for all orders

Role Simulation

Situation

The students are asked to imagine that their boss is ill. Several visitors arrive in the office that day and it is the secretary's job to deal with them. The students should agree upon a name for the boss.

Preparation		The teacher should study the roles given below and draw up his own roles.
		It is suggested that for Roles 5, 8 and 9 the teacher should arrange for a telephone on the secretary's 'desk' to enable her to make the imaginary phone calls.
Procedure		The students take it in turn to play the part of secretary and each pupil should be given a copy of one of the roles.

They should:
1. establish or confirm the identity of the visitor
2. introduce themselves and explain the situation
3. answer polite enquiries about the boss's health
4. deal with the visitor as indicated
5. answer any questions the visitor may ask them

The teacher should play the role of visitor throughout. In some cases he will have to invent certain facts such as name and purpose of his visit. He should also ask the secretary questions whenever the opportunity arises. The teacher should begin each role simulation with: 'Is this Mr . . .'s office?'

Secretary's Roles

1. Confirm that the visitor is a Mr Rankin who has an appointment. Introduce yourself and explain the situation. (Invent an illness.) Answer his polite enquiry. Tell him that another member of staff (invent a name) will see him instead and give him directions to get to that person's office on a different floor.

2. This caller is unknown to you so you must first establish his identity, and find out whether your boss was expecting him. Introduce yourself and explain the situation. (Invent an illness.) Answer his polite enquiry. Find out what he has called about. Suggest someone else in the company who may be able to help him.

3. This caller introduces himself and asks to see your boss. He explains the purpose of his visit briefly. Introduce yourself and explain the situation. (Invent an illness.) Answer his polite enquiry. Offer to find the documents he has come to collect and ask him what they were about. Tell him you know where they are and ask him to wait a minute. When you have got them explain that your boss hasn't signed them yet. Offer to post the documents to him when they are signed and get his address.

4. Confirm that the visitor is a Mr Phillips who has an appointment. Introduce yourself and explain the situation. (Invent an illness.) Answer his polite enquiry. Tell him that you have arranged for him to see your boss's assistant. (Invent a name.) Confirm if this is all right and when he seems doubtful assure him that the assistant has the authority to deal with the matter. Offer to take him to the assistant's room.

Role Simulation

5. Confirm that the visitor is a Mr Gray who has an appointment. Introduce yourself and explain the situation. (Invent an illness.) Answer his polite enquiry. Confirm that he has come to sign a contract. Tell him that someone in the legal department will see him. (Invent a name.) Excuse yourself then hold an imaginary telephone conversation with the person in the legal department, telling him of the visitor's arrival. After the call, explain that the person will come immediately to collect him.

6. This caller is unknown to you, so you must first establish his identity. Introduce yourself and explain the situation. (Invent an illness.) Answer his polite enquiry. Try and arrange an appointment for him to see your boss. The first time you mention is not acceptable to him, so ask him when it would be convenient.

7. Confirm that the visitor is a Mr Thompson who has a lunch appointment. Introduce yourself and explain the situation. (Invent an illness.) Answer his polite enquiry. Tell him that one of your boss's colleagues will take him to lunch. (Invent a name.) This person is still at a meeting and will not be ready for about half an hour. Apologize for the delay. In reply to his enquiry, tell him something about the position of the colleague. Suggest something he could do while he's waiting.

8. This caller introduces himself and asks to see your boss. Introduce yourself and explain the situation. (Invent an illness.) Answer his polite enquiry. Find out if you can help in any way and ask what he has called about. Suggest someone who might be able to provide him with the information he wants and then conduct an imaginary telephone conversation with that person and relay the information to the visitor.

9. This caller is a Mr Pendred and he is already well known to you. Greet him and ask him about his health and his journey. Explain the situation. (Invent an illness.) Apologize for not having been able to get in touch with him to warn him. Ask him who else he would like to see instead. When he has told you, conduct an imaginary telephone conversation with that person. Confirm that a meeting can be arranged but only after lunch. Suggest that he uses the company canteen and direct him there.

10. This caller introduces himself and asks to see your boss. Introduce yourself and explain the situation. (Invent an illness.) The caller is very anxious to know when your boss will be back and you speculate on a possible date. Ask him if there's anyone else he would like to see instead and when he says no, offer to make an appointment for a future date. Discuss with him a convenient time and offer to phone him to confirm the appointment. Get his telephone number and find out what his business is.

Key to 'What is this?'

Page 45: 1 dial   2 receiver   3 transfer button
Page 47: cash box
Page 49: safe

Unit 5

Unit Summary

Introductory Recording
This episode is entitled 'A Death to Report'. Mary Malone hears of the death of Arne Jensen, the Production Manager of one of Schweibur's associate companies. She has to find out the details of his life so that an obituary can be put in the company journal.

Text
The Text is the obituary that appears in the company journal.

Vocabulary
Exercise A is a two-part exercise on vocabulary which appears in the Text.

Structures
1 Past reference (Exercise B and Drill 1)
Past simple / Past perfect

Mr Jensen *died* last Sunday.
He *had spent* many years in the service of Andersen Ltd.

2 Phrasal verbs with *take* (Exercise C and Drill 2)

Pronunciation Practice
This deals with the difference between the vowel sounds [ɪ] as in *tin*, [e] as in *ten*, [ɜ] as in *turn* and [ʌ] as in *ton*. There is an ear-training exercise followed by repetition of a limerick.

Dialogue
The situation is that of a secretary checking the arrangements for a visit.

Correspondence
There is a draft letter to be corrected.

Telegrams
There are four telegrams: two to be decoded and two to be encoded.

Gambits
Drill 3: Apologizing.
*I'm so sorry to hear . . . , Mr . . . . Please accept our apologies.
I'll ask Mr Heine to . . . .*

Drill 4: Handling enquiries that cannot be answered immediately.
I can't tell you . . . offhand, I'm afraid. But if you'd like to hold on a moment, I'll . . . .

Active Listening
There are three passages in this unit.
1 A telephone conversation with a request for action.
2 A telephone message. The student has to answer comprehension questions.
3 Comprehension of a recorded instruction.

Unit Summary

Role Simulation

The students are asked to imagine that a visitor to their company has come to them for help in dealing with a problem. The teacher is required to play the part of the visitor throughout. There are roles for both the teacher and the students.

Homework

The written gambit introduced in the unit deals with:

Expressing dissatisfaction and complaining.

Introductory Recording

Tapescript

A Death to Report

Schweibur issues a monthly journal called the Schweibur Gazette. It is edited by Mr Müller and his staff. And the other day Mary Malone went to Mr Müller's office to ask him about something.

Müller: Ah, good morning, Miss Malone.

Malone: Good morning, Mr Müller. How are you?

Müller: As well as can be expected. Under pressure as usual. We don't see you very often. What can we do for you?

Müller: Oh, Miss Malone. That's the phone near you. I wonder, I'm very busy. Will you take that, please?

Malone: Yes, of course. Hello, Mr Müller's office, can I help you?

Receptionist: There's a call for Mr Müller. Mr Nording, of Andersen's Copenhagen. Will you take it?

Malone: Just a moment, please. Mr Müller, it's Nording. The Managing Director at Andersen's. Shall I take it?

Müller: Yes, do, please. And take any message down, will you?

Malone: Yes, of course. Hello? Put Mr Nording through, please.

Nording: Hello. Nording here.

Malone: Good morning, Mr Nording. This is Mary Malone.

Nording: Oh. Erm. Well, I'm rather surprised to hear your voice, Miss Malone. Are you not working for Mr Gräber any longer? Have you taken up journalism?

Malone: Oh no, Mr Nording. Nothing like that. I'm just visiting the Gazette office.

Nording: Oh I see. Well, I was expecting to speak to Mr Müller.

Malone: Actually, he's rather busy at the moment. He asked me to take the call.

Nording: Yes, I see. Well, it's rather sad news I'm afraid. I have to report the death at Andersen's of one of our staff. He passed away at the weekend. And I know Mr Müller usually puts an, erm, obituary in the Gazette on these occasions. So I . . .

Malone: Oh dear, I am sorry to hear that. Is it someone . . .

Nording: I'm not sure if you knew him. It's our Mr Jensen, Production . . .

Malone: What, Arne Jensen? The Production Manager?

Nording: Yes, that's right. You knew him?

Malone: Well, yes I did. Oh dear, I'm quite taken aback. I was speaking to him earlier this month, in fact. And he came to our 50th anniversary. Oh dear, such a pleasant man. He wasn't very old, surely?

Nording: No. Only 53. It is very sad. But he had some heart trouble. He'd been having treatment for it. But he took so much work on always. He tried to do too much, I think.

Malone: Oh dear. When did he actually . . .

Nording: Um, it was on Sunday evening. He and his family . . . *(Fade)*

Nording: So Miss Frederiksen will take over his work temporarily. And now I'd better ring off. There's a lot to do. Goodbye, Miss Malone.

Malone: Yes, goodbye Mr Nording. I'll tell Mr Müller. And thank you for ringing. Goodbye. Did you know Mr Jensen had heart trouble, Mr Müller?

Müller: Erm, I hardly knew him really. But I'm sorry to hear this news of him. So. I must prepare the obituary. Have you got the, er, details there?

Malone: Yes. But I thought I'd get some more information from Miss Walter in Personnel. I know Mr Gräber will want to write a letter of condolence. So I'll make some notes to take up to him, and give you a copy too. May I ring her from here?

Müller: Yes, yes, of course, go ahead.

Malone: Hello: Personnel? Oh, it's about . . . *(Fade)*

Malone: So if you can give me some of those details. Where he was born, how long he'd been with the company, and so on.

Walter: Yes, I see. Well. I'm afraid I can't tell you offhand. Will you hold the line a moment? I'll get the file. Hold on. . . . Now, here we are. Mr Jensen . . . *(Fade)*

Walter: . . . And he'd been with Andersen's 20 years last January.

Malone: And what positions had he held?

Walter: Erm, let's see. He started as Workshop Foreman. Promoted

Introductory Recording 77

Assistant Production Manager 1965. And took over as Head of Production last year.

Malone: Right, I've got that. Now. Any special points I need to mention?

Walter: Erm, yes. He had been a member of the Danish Association of Production Engineers for nine years. And I suppose his normal duties at Andersen's took up most of his time, but he had also, it seems, been developing an interest in workshop safety. He had made some important improvements at Andersen's which other companies have been copying, it says here.

Malone: Oh, fine. That's very useful. I'll ring back if there's anything else I think of. It's very sad, isn't it?

Walter: Yes, indeed. And goodbye, Miss Malone.

Malone: Yes, goodbye. And thank you. I've got the information, now, Mr Müller, so if you . . . *(Fade)*

Comprehension Questions

1. Whose office was Mary in?
   Mr Müller's

2. What does Mr Müller do?
   He produces the Schweibur Gazette.

3. What was the telephone call Mary took about?
   The death of Arne Jensen in Copenhagen.

4. What does Müller have to do?
   Write an obituary in the Gazette.

5. Where does Mary go for more information about Arne Jensen?
   Miss Walter in Personnel.

6. Why does she want this information?
   So that Mr Gräber can write a letter (of condolence).

7. How did Mary react to Jensen's death?
   She was surprised and sad.

Text: A Death to Report

The words and phrases in italics are quoted verbatim from the Text.

Comprehension Questions

1. Where did Jensen die?
   At his home on the outskirts of Copenhagen.

2. When did he die?
   He *died on 10th July.*

3   What sort of career did Mr Jensen have?
    He *had a long and distinguished* one.

4   What was he passionately interested in?
    All aspects of the company's activities.

5   Did he gain quick promotion within the company?
    Yes, he did.

6   When was he appointed Assistant Production Manager?
    In 1965.

7   How long before that had he joined the company?
    He *had joined it only eleven years before.*

8   What did he pioneer as Assistant Production Manager?
    A number of new production processes.

9   What did Mr Jensen's work during this period lead to?
    It lead to Schweibur's achievement of a dominant position in a number of fields.

10 Had he been a member of the Association of Engineers before 1965?
    No, he hadn't.

11 How long did he hold the position of President?
    From *1970 until his death.*

12 For how long had he been Assistant Production Manager before his promotion?
    He had been Assistant Production Manager for nine years.

13 What did he immediately implement?
    A great many improvements in production techniques.

14 What did these lead to?
    Andersen's becoming a showpiece of industrial efficiency.

15 For how long had he had an interest in industrial safety?
    For *a great many years.*

16 What had his interest led to by 1965?
    It had led to Andersen's achieving one of the best safety records in Denmark.

17 What had his innovations produced by 1973?
    They had produced the lowest accident rate of any company in Europe.

18 What did his friends in Zurich value in him?
    His *many personal qualities and bubbling humour.*

19 How will his friends remember him?
    With affection and gratitude.

Key to the Exercises

Exercise A

1. He had a long and *distinguished* career.
2. In 1965 he was *elected* a member of the DAPE.
3. He *held* that post until he died.
4. It was with *profound* regret that we learnt of the death of . . .

passionate interest
rapid promotion
deepest sympathy
bubbling humour

Exercise B

1. He had worked for the company for 20 years when he retired.
2. Your telex reached us after we had already despatched your order.
3. We offered to replace the machine but the customer had already gone to another supplier.
4. He acted very quickly once he had made up his mind.
5. He had already served his apprenticeship before he joined the company.
6. We had just insured against fire when one broke out.
7. The late Mr Smith had edited the company journal for five years before his resignation in 1972.
8. He had already left Schweibur when he went to Brazil.

Exercise C

Possible answers

1. Yesterday some visitors *were taken round* the factory.
2. The secretary had some difficulty *taking down* the minutes.
3. The Vice-President *took over* when the President died.
4. All motorists are obliged *to take out* an insurance policy.
5. We would like *to take up* Spanish.
6. The chairman asked him *to take back* his remarks.
7. I don't envy the person who *takes on* that job.
8. He was very *taken aback* by the tragedy.
9. We were all *taken in* by his false promises.
10. They say he *took to* drink.

Language Laboratory Part 1: Tapescript

Drill 1

Mr Schulz, the Personnel Manager at Schweibur, is talking about the late Mr Jensen. He has difficulty in remembering what things Mr Jensen did and his secretary has to correct some of his statements.

1. (Example) Poor Jensen. Such a tragedy. We were just going to promote him to Head of Production, weren't we?
No, he had been Head of Production since last March.

2 (Example) Yes, now I remember. Wasn't he trying to complete the expansion programme when he took over?
No, he had completed the expansion programme by 1972.

3 Ah, yes, so he had. 1972, that was when we made him Assistant Production Manager, wasn't it?
No, he had been Assistant Production Manager since 1965.

4 That was the first post he's held, wasn't it?
No, he had held the post of Workshop Foreman for several years.

5 Oh, had he? Now, that must have been shortly after leaving the Finn Company.
No, he had left the Finn Company by 1954.

6 Really! As early as that. Now, didn't he work in Africa at some time?
No, he had worked in Brazil before that.

7 Ah, yes, now I remember. That was where he developed that new technique with hardwood.
No, he developed that new technique before he went there.

8 Oh, yes, of course, he must have. And he was still doing his apprenticeship during the war.
No, he had done his apprenticeship by 1940.

Drill 2

Miss Walter and Miss Wood are gossiping in the office.

1 (Example) I heard that Mr Shermann is retiring. Do you know who is replacing him?
I understand Mr Fromm is taking over.

2 (Example) I don't think this covers us against fire. Who arranged this insurance policy?
I understand Mr Braun took it out.

3 Your boss seems to be very interested in languages. What's he studying now?
I understand he's taken up Russian.

4 I see we have a party of visitors this afternoon. Is anyone showing them the factory?
I understand Maureen's taking them round.

5 Being Secretary to the Staff Association is a lot of extra work. Who is going to have that responsibility?
I understand Ann is going to take it on.

6 I thought Mr Flügel was very rude to Frieda. I hope he apologized.
I understand he took back his remarks.

7 This telephone message is not at all clear. D'you know who wrote it?
I understand Franz took it down.

	8 Mr Flügel looks as though he's had a nasty surprise. What's wrong? *I understand he was taken aback by Frieda's resignation.*

Pronunciation Practice

In this unit we're going to study four vowel sounds. Listen to the example words that are given in your book.

1 *tin*

2 *ten*

3 *turn*

4 *ton*

Which one is this?

ton

That was number four. And this one?

tin

That was number one. Now we're going to say ten words. Listen carefully and decide whether the word has the vowel sound of example one, two, three or four and then write the number down. Are you ready? Listen carefully.

1	*bud*	6	*lurk*
2	*pert*	7	*fill*
3	*bin*	8	*fussed*
4	*deck*	9	*curse*
5	*fern*	10	*head*

Now here are the correct answers.

One was number four	Six was number three
Two was number three	Seven was number one
Three was number one	Eight was number four
Four was number two	Nine was number three
Five was number three	Ten was number two

Did you get most of these right? Now let's practise the pronunciation of these sounds. Look at the limerick in your book. Listen to it first.

There once was a typist called Shirley,
Who worked for a boss who was surly.
He was stingy and bitter,
And would never permit her
To come late or go away early.

Now repeat this limerick line by line. Pay attention to the example vowel sounds and to the long, loud syllables printed in capitals.

Dialogue

The Production Manager is expecting a visit from a Mr Davidson from the English company, Gosbecks Ltd. He has asked Miss Jones, his secretary, to ring up and check when Mr Davidson will be coming.

Switchboard: Gosbecks Ltd.

Miss Jones: Good morning. Could you put me through to Mr Davidson's office, please.

Switchboard: Hold the line please.

Secretary: Mr Davidson's office.

Miss Jones: Good morning. I'm Mr Shermann's secretary at Schweibur.

Secretary: Oh, good morning. What can we do for you?

Miss Jones: I'd just like to ask you about Mr Davidson's visit on Thursday. I wonder if you could tell me what time he's arriving?

Secretary: Just a moment, I've got a note of this. Yes, he'll be arriving at about eleven o'clock.

Miss Jones: And I understand he'll be spending the rest of the day here.

Secretary: Yes, that's what he had in mind anyway.

Miss Jones: Fine. We look forward to seeing him then. Thank you very much.

Secretary: Goodbye.

Correspondence

In this Key suggestions for an acceptable version are printed in bold type.

Dear Mr Hofmeyer,

We were **deeply distressed** to learn of the tragic **death** of Mr Kaltenbrunner in a car accident last week. We have always had the highest regard for Mr Kaltenbrunner throughout his long **association** with our company, and his loss **will be keenly / deeply felt**. Many of us **feel** that we **have lost** not just a business associate, but a **close** personal friend.

On behalf of our company please **convey** our deepest **sympathy** and **sincere condolences to his wife and family in their loss**.

Yours sincerely,

Telegrams

There is a strike at Nigerian ports. All orders for Lagos should be airfreighted.

Because we are now ordering a smaller number of goods you should only send one lorry each week.

1   GENOA STEAMER CIRCA FIFTEENTH CANCELLED STOP MUST SHIP YOUR ORDER ONE SIX ZERO PER MS MARCO POLO SAILING NAPLES CIRCA TWENTYFIRST STOP

2   OWING LOW QUOTATION REGRET IMPOSSIBLE FIVE PER CENT DISCOUNT ON ORDERS UNDER FIFTY THOUSAND PAPERCLIPS STOP HOLDING YOUR ORDER PENDING CONFIRMATION STOP

Language Laboratory Part 2: Tapescript

Drill 3

Miss Wood is secretary to Mr Heine, Sales Manager of Schweibur. Customers sometimes ring the Sales Department to make complaints and Miss Wood has to apologize to them.

1   (Example)   Stenberg speaking. I'd like to know why our order hasn't arrived.
I'm sorry to hear your order hasn't arrive, Mr Stenberg. Please accept our apologies.

2   (Example)   My name's Brown. I'm ringing to let you know our goods are damaged. This isn't good enough, you know.
I'm sorry to hear your goods are damaged, Mr Brown. Please accept our apologies.

3   Lebrun here. About this invoice you sent us; you've overcharged us, I'm afraid.
I'm sorry to hear we've overcharged you, Mr Lebrun. Please accept our apologies.

4   Hallo? Sales Department? This is Rossi speaking. You've sent us the wrong consignment. This is the second time it's happened.
I'm sorry to hear we've sent you the wrong consignment, Mr Rossi. Please accept our apologies.

Now it isn't good enough just to apologize when someone makes a complaint. Miss Wood has to tell the customer what she is going to do to put matters right.

1   (Example)   Stenberg speaking. I'd like to know why our order hasn't arrived.
I'm sorry to hear your order hasn't arrived, Mr Stenberg. Please accept our apologies. I'll ask Mr Heine to look into the matter.

2 (Example) My name's Brown. I'm ringing to let you know our goods are damaged. This isn't good enough, you know.
I'm sorry to hear your goods are damaged, Mr Brown. Please accept our apologies. I'll ask Mr Heine to attend to it immediately.

3 Lebrun here. About this invoice you sent us; you've overcharged us, I'm afraid.
I'm sorry to hear we've overcharged you, Mr Lebrun. Please accept our apologies. I'll ask Mr Heine to take the matter up with our accounts department.

4 Hullo? Sales Department? This is Rossi speaking. You've sent us the wrong consignment. This is the second time it's happened.
I'm sorry to hear we've sent you the wrong consignment, Mr Rossi. Please accept our apologies. I'll ask Mr Heine to make enquiries immediately.

5 Nelson here. For God's sake will you get a move on with those spare parts. They still haven't arrived.
I'm sorry to hear the spare parts still haven't arrived, Mr Nelson. Please accept our apologies. I'll ask Mr Heine to look into the matter immediately.

6 My name is Steuermann. You never replied to my letter.
I'm sorry to hear we never replied to your letter, Mr Steuermann. Please accept our apologies. I'll ask Mr Heine to attend to the matter straight away.

7 My name is van Stunk. We weren't informed about the price increases. What the hell are you playing at?
I'm sorry to hear you weren't informed about the price increase, Mr van Stunk. Please accept our apologies. I'll ask Mr Heine to take the matter up at once.

8 Da Silva here. I'm ringing to complain about our recent order. The goods are poor quality, I'm afraid. Can you replace them as soon as possible please?
I'm sorry to hear the goods are poor quality, Mr da Silva. Please accept our apologies. I'll ask Mr Heine to sort this out as soon as possible.

Drill 4

Sometimes when her boss is away Miss Wood receives enquiries which she is not able to answer immediately.

1 (Example) Betty, when is our new manual coming out?
I can't tell you when it's coming out offhand, I'm afraid.

2 (Example) Miss Wood, how much discount did we allow Markhams Ltd?
I can't tell you how much we allowed offhand, I'm afraid.

3 Betty, what is our new reference number for Perkins Ltd?
I can't tell you what it is offhand, I'm afraid.

4   Ah, Miss Wood. The exhibition next month. When does it open?
    I can't tell you when it opens offhand, I'm afraid.

Now it is not usually enough for a secretary to say that she can't answer the caller's enquiry. She also has to tell the caller what she is going to do to help him find out what he wants to know.

1   (Example)   Betty, when is our new manual coming out?
    I can't tell you when it's coming out offhand, I'm afraid. But if you'd like to hold on a moment, I'll put you through to the editor.

2   (Example)   Miss Wood, how much discount did we allow Markhams Ltd?
    I can't tell you how much we allowed offhand, I'm afraid. But if you'd like to hold on a moment, I'll check through the correspondence.

3   Betty, what is our new reference number for Perkins Ltd?
    I can't tell you what it is offhand, I'm afraid. But if you'd like to hold on a moment, I'll look it up in our customers' index.

4   Ah, Miss Wood. The exhibition next month. When does it open?
    I can't tell you when it opens offhand, I'm afraid. But if you'd like to hold on a moment, I'll check in Mr Heine's diary.

5   That meeting next week, Miss Wood. Is it in the blue room, or the red one?
    I can't tell you where it is offhand, I'm afraid. But if you'd like to hold on a moment, I'll find out for you.

6   Betty, you know this reception at the Grand Hotel, are we all going together, or making our own way there?
    I can't tell you how we're going offhand, I'm afraid. But if you'd like to hold on a moment, I'll see if anyone knows.

7   Miss Wood, when did we send invoice number F3417 to Smiths?
    I can't tell you when we sent it offhand. But if you'd like to hold on a moment, I'll consult our records for you.

8   Mr Farouk's secretary. Now, you put our order on SS Minerva at Genoa but you didn't tell us what the sailing time was. What was it in fact?
    I can't tell you what it was offhand, I'm afraid. But if you'd like to hold on a moment I'll put you through to Mr Boileau in the transport department.

Active Listening

Passage 1: Mr Heine has gone to Austria for a sales conference. He rings his secretary, Miss Wood, from Vienna.

Miss Wood: Mr Heine's office.

Mr Heine: Hallo, Heine here. Thank you for sending those papers, by the way. I wonder if you could ring the Head Storeman and get some information for me? What I want to know fairly urgently is how many executive desks, Model TT3 we have in stock, and how soon we could deliver fifty units to Hoffmann's of Vienna.

Miss Wood: Yes, I'll ring you back as soon as possible. Goodbye.

Mr Heine: Goodbye.

What does Mr Heine want Miss Wood to do?
He wants her to ring the Head Storeman, and find out how many executive desks, Model TT3, there are in stock and how soon 50 could be delivered to Hoffmann's of Vienna.

Passage 2: Miss Miller works for the Training Manager of Schweibur, Mr Konstanz. Yesterday, when Mr Konstanz was not in the office, Miss Miller received the following message:

Miss Miller: Mr Konstanz's office, can I help you?

Allen: Allen speaking, Institute of Management, London. Is Konstanz there?

Miss Miller: I'm afraid he isn't, Mr Allen. Can I help you at all?

Allen: I'm sure you could. It's about the training course we're giving for you in a fortnight's time. I have a note of equipment we shall need for this in front of me, and was wondering if Mr Konstanz could arrange for it to be available.

Miss Miller: If you'd like to let me know what you need, Mr Allen, I'll see that Mr Konstanz is informed.

Allen: Fine. We'll need two tape recorders, an overhead projector, and if possible a slide projector.

Miss Miller: Fine.

Allen: And from day 3 onwards we'll need two rooms, as we'll be dividing the participants into two groups. The rest we'll bring ourselves, of course.

Miss Miller: Thank you. I'll tell Mr Konstanz as soon as he's back.

Allen: Thank you so much. Goodbye.

Miss Miller: Goodbye.

1. Who wants to speak to Mr Konstanz?
   Mr *Allen*, from the *Institute of Management, London.*

2. What is he ringing up about?
   The *training course* taking place *in a fortnight's time.*

3. What does he have in front of him?
   A note of the equipment he *will need.*

4   What equipment will be needed?
    Two tape recorders, an overhead projector and if possible a slide projector.

5   When will two rooms be needed?
    From day 3 onwards.

6   Why?
    Because *the participants* will be divided *into two groups.*

7   Now write down the message Miss Miller should give Mr Konstanz.
    Mr Allen from the Institute of Management, London, rang about the training course taking place in a fortnight's time. He will need two tape recorders, an overhead projector and, if possible, a slide projector. From day 3 onwards he will need 2 rooms because the participants will be divided into 2 groups.

Passage 3: Your boss is not in this morning. He has recorded a message on the dictaphone. Listen to it and then answer the question in your book.

Letter to Mrs Andersson expressing our sympathy, er, death of her husband. Draft this one, would you, and let me have a look at it before it goes.

What do you have to do?
Draft a letter of sympathy to Mrs Andersson. Let the boss see it before it is sent.

Role Simulation

Situation	The students are asked to imagine that a visitor to their company has come to them for help in dealing with a problem.
Preparation	The teacher should study the roles given below and draw up his own roles for the part of the visitor.
Procedure	The teacher should play the role of the visitor throughout. Guidelines as to the nature of the problem are given below. After hearing the problem, the secretary should:

express her willingness to help
question the visitor in order to obtain all the information she needs to deal with the request.

Each student should be given one of the roles which consist of reminders as to what they should ask. |
| Roles | 1 **Visitor:** Look, can you help me? I must have left my briefcase somewhere. I know I had it when I arrived here this morning. |

Secretary: colour—size—material of briefcase—any initials/label on it—movements of visitor since he arrived this morning.

2 **Visitor:** Look, can you help me? I'd like to get hold of a hire car.

Secretary: length of hire—starting time—expected mileage—delivery instructions—handing back instructions—preferred make of car—any special model/fittings—driving licence—costing before accepting?

3 **Visitor:** Look, can you help me? I've just discovered that I've left some important documents behind in my office. I'll need these later this week. I wonder if you could phone them up and get them to send them on?

Secretary: phone number—name of secretary or colleague/extension? description of documents—subject matter—where can they be found—posting instructions—address.

4 **Visitor:** Look, can you help me? I've got to make an unexpected trip to . . . , calling at . . . on the way, and then I want to come back here. I was wondering if you could make the necessary arrangements for me?

Secretary: air/rail/sea?—class—departure date—morning/afternoon? time to be spent at first place—time of arrival at second place—length of time there—time of return journey—accommodation on trip?

5 **Visitor:** Look, can you help me? I'm going to be tied up with business meetings over the weekend and won't be able to get to the shops. I wonder if you could possibly get some presents for my kids on Saturday. (Three: souvenir for teenager; toy for 7 year old; clothes for baby.)

Secretary: number of children—ages—kind of present?—toys/books/clothes/souvenirs?—interests of children—sizes—price limit.

6 **Visitor:** Look, can you help me? I've got this report to be typed. D'you think you could manage it?

Secretary: size of paper—number of copies—typing instructions about spacing/underlining of headings/etc.—when required—where he can be reached if there are any queries—circulation list.

7 **Visitor:** Look, can you help me? I discovered this morning that my car was broken into last night and a suitcase had been stolen. I've got this urgent meeting to go to. Could you deal with the police for me?

Secretary: place of theft—time of theft—how did the thieves break into the car—description of suitcase—list of contents—value.

8 **Visitor:** Look, can you help me? I've been staying with Mr and Mrs . . . all week and they've been extremely good to me. I'd like to return their

hospitality by taking them out, say to the theatre and for a meal. A really good night on the town. I wonder if you could do the bookings for me? I don't even know what's on or where to go.

Secretary: what night—what kind of show—what is the taste of his guests—what type of seats—prices—meal before or after—what kind of restaurant—how many people altogether?

9 **Visitor:** Look, can you help me? I was supposed to be meeting someone off a plane at 7, but I've been held up here. I want to get a message to him to tell him to go straight to the hotel.

Secretary: name of person—time of arrival—from where—airline—flight number—which hotel—when and where will he meet the person?

10 **Visitor:** Look, can you help me? I'd very much like to have a tour of the company before I leave and speak to a number of other people. D'you think you could fix up a programme for me?

Secretary: what does he want to see—who does he want to speak to—what does he want to talk to them about—about how long does he want to spend at each place/with each person—in what order does he want to do these things?

Key to 'What is this?'

Page 58: envelopes, headed notepaper, plain paper (continuation sheets); stationery

Unit 6

Unit Summary

Introductory Recording	This episode is entitled 'A Visitor'. Mr Gräber has been delayed at a meeting and Mary Malone has to look after a visitor until he returns.
Text	The Text is a Memo which has been drawn up as a result of this meeting between Mr Gräber and the visitor.
Vocabulary	Exercise A is a three-part exercise on vocabulary which appears in the Text.
Structures	1 The passive voice of: (Exercise B and Drill 1) present simple present continuous future simple past simple present perfect past perfect *Would/should* (Exercise C and Drill 2)
Pronunciation Practice	This deals with the difference between the vowel sounds [ɪə] as in *beer*, [eə] as in *bear* and [eɪ] as in *bay*. There is an ear-training exercise followed by repetition of a limerick.
Dialogue	The situation is that of dealing with a complaint from a customer (as in Unit 2). It is a five-stage dialogue, in which practice of alternative expressions is introduced.
Correspondence	There is a draft letter to be corrected.
Telegrams	There are four telegrams, two to be decoded and two to be encoded.
Gambits	Drill 3: Suggesting. *If you . . . , you might like to . . .* Drill 4: Asking for details. *I'm afraid I haven't heard anything about . . .*
Active Listening	There are two passages in this unit. 1 Comprehension of a telephone message. 2 A dictated letter to be written down in full.

Unit Summary

Role Simulation

The students are asked to imagine that a visitor has arrived fifteen minutes too early for an appointment with their boss. To pass the time while he is waiting the visitor starts up a conversation. The secretary has to respond and keep the conversation going. Roles are provided for the teacher, who plays the part of the visitor throughout.

Homework

The written gambit introduced in this unit deals with:

Polite refusals to requests and excuses.

Introductory Recording

Tapescript

A Visitor

While Mary Malone is working in her office one morning, a visitor arrives to see her boss, Erich Gräber. But he has been delayed at a meeting, so Mary has to look after the visitor until he returns.

Malone: Mr Gräber's office.

Receptionist: Reception here, Miss Malone. I have a Mrs dos Santos to see Mr Gräber.

Malone: Oh yes. Will you ask her to come up, please?

Receptionist: Yes, certainly.

Malone: Thank you.

Malone: Good morning, Mrs dos Santos.

Santos: Ah, good morning, nice to see you again.

Malone: Very nice to see you, too.

Santos: Oh, thank you. But, erm, this is not the office I came to before, surely?

Malone: No, you're quite right. Our other office is being redecorated and we have just been moved here temporarily. It's not really very convenient. But we're hoping it won't be for very long.

Santos: Oh, I know, it's dreadful when you have to move office. Terrible. Er, Mr Gräber, is he in? I have an appointment . . .

Malone: Yes, he is expecting you, of course, but I'm sorry, he's not here at the moment. He's been held up at one of his meetings. He called ten minutes ago. Can you wait a few minutes? Would you like a table to work at while you wait?

Santos: Well, I suppose I should work. But I don't think I will, not for a few minutes only.

Malone: Oh, fine. Erm, have you come a long way this time?

Santos: Well, I've been travelling all over Europe for three weeks now, almost non-stop.

Malone: Sounds rather exciting. Where have you been?

Santos: Oh, I've been visiting most of the branches, looking at the various design centres and departments that we have. You know. And it's very interesting, of course, but, you know, when you're moving around like this all the time and you're always in planes and you're eating so many meals, you get, you know, quite dazed.

Malone: Yes, I'm sure you do. Though sometimes I think I'd rather like it. But you should be able to relax a bit with us. Do you think you'll be visiting the Schweibur workshops in Zurich?

Santos: Oh, yes. I'm going to see them this afternoon. Miss Lachenal . . . you know . . . ?

Malone: Yes, I know.

Santos: . . . she should be giving me a guided tour round the design section this afternoon.

Malone: Oh, that's good.

Santos: Very interesting things are being produced here, you know.

Malone: Yes, aren't there? And, er, where else have you, er . . .

Santos: Well, Denmark. I visited Copenhagen and spent quite a time there, and, oh, it was most interesting. I was very impressed. Of course, the Danes are famous for their designs.

Malone: Have you been to Ireland at all?

Santos: Yes, I have. Are you from there?

Malone: Well I was born there. Did you get to Dublin?

Santos: Ah, I was only there for one night. It was a stopover, you know, on my way from New York to Europe. But I've got some friends in Ireland and I'd been invited to stay for three days. Such a pity, I did want to stay. Such a beautiful country, you know.

Malone: Oh, it is, yes.

Santos: But we've got this, er schedule to keep to and there just wasn't enough time.

Malone: Oh, that's a shame. Still, perhaps you'll go back one day for a holiday.

Santos: Oh, I would like to very, very much. But you know how it is. Work comes first. Ah. Perhaps I may be able to get there after the international conference. I hear it may be held in Dublin. Do you know anything about it?

Malone: No, no, I'm afraid I haven't heard anything about it. When is it being planned for?

Santos: Well, I'm surprised you haven't been informed. It's supposed to be held in the first half of next year. It was intended to hold it in Caracas, but we wouldn't have the staff available at that time, you know. So I understand they've changed it to Dublin. So I might get that holiday . . .

Malone: Oh, that would be great. Oh, by the way, Mrs Santos. Do you know Mrs Sanchez?

Santos: Mrs Sanchez? I should know her. We've been working together for ten years or more. Why?

Malone: Well, she was here for the fiftieth anniversary. I was just hoping she got back alright. She was a little worried, I think, about her trip.

Santos: Oh yes, she would be. Always worried about everything. Yes, she got back, not on the right plane, but she got back, and do you know, she had to pay something like $200 excess baggage. She bought so many presents to bring back.

Malone: Oh, good gracious, poor soul. But do give her my regards when you see her, will you?

Santos: Yes, yes, I will, of course.

Gräber: Ah, Mrs Santos. It's very good to see you again. I'm sorry I'm late. Been delayed by the Chief Accountant. I'm always being delayed by the Chief Accountant. He just never stops asking questions, does he, Mary?

Santos: Yes, but where would be without accountants?

Gräber: Yes, you're right, of course. Anyway, how are you? How was the journey? You've come such a long way to see us.

Santos: Oh, I'm very well indeed. And I've been having a very good trip. Mind you, there's an awful lot to do, a very crowded schedule. But it's all been very, very interesting and, er, I've been very well looked after by Mary here.

Gräber: I'm sure you have. Well done, Mary. Now, you will come in, yes? Mary, would you come in too, please. We shall need notes of our discussion. And there'll be a memo to be circulated afterwards. Will you follow me?

Santos: Yes. You know, you should let Mary visit us in Caracas some time . . . *(Fade)*

Comprehension Questions

1 Why couldn't Mr Gräber see Mrs dos Santos immediately?
  He'd been held up at a meeting.

94   Unit 6

2   What has Mrs dos Santos been doing for the past three weeks?
    Travelling all over Europe.

3   Why did she visit most of the branches?
    To look at the various design centres.

4   What is her attitude to all this travelling?
    Although it's very interesting she doesn't like moving around so much. She says she's quite dazed.

5   Which of her visits impressed her a lot?
    Her visit to Copenhagen.

6   Why was she disappointed about her trip to Ireland?
    She'd been invited to stay (for three days) with friends but there wasn't time to stay for more than one night.

7   When does Mrs dos Santos hope to visit Ireland again?
    At the next international conference.

8   Can you remember the name of the person whom both women know?
    Mrs Sanchez.

9   What does Mary Malone want to know about Mrs Sanchez?
    If she got back alright after her visit for the fiftieth anniversary.

10 When Mr Gräber comes in, who does he blame for the delay?
    The Chief Accountant.

Text: A Memo

Comprehension Questions

The words and phrases in italics are quoted verbatim from the Text.

1   What has been submitted by the Research Section in Caracus?
    The final design for the Fonacopy facsimile transceiver.

2   What can be done with this machine?
    Virtually any drawn, photographed, typed or written document can be sent or received *over public or private telephone lines.*

3   What has Schweibur's Market Research Department spent much of the last three months doing?
    Estimating the size of the market for the Fonacopy.

4   What is attached to this Memo?
    The *final report on* the Fonacopy / *this subject.*

5   What else is attached?
    The conclusions they *have drawn and the objectives* they *propose.*

6   What can be done after 1978?
    A large market for the Fonacopy can be developed.

Introductory Recording

7 How big is the present market in Europe for the Fonacopy?
It is essentially limited to two hundred major potential customers.

8 What does Mr Gräber's Department recommend?
That the quantities it is proposed to produce in 1977 should be revised.

9 Where are the amendments to the existing production estimates?
They *are set out in Appendix C.*

10 When will production capacity have to be increased?
As demand for this type of equipment is developed over the coming years.

11 Is Schweibur the only company to have developed such a product?
No, it isn't. *Similar products have already been developed by three companies in the UK and the United States.*

12 What must be done if Schweibur is to succeed with this product?
This market competition will have to be faced and an acceptable share of the market won.

13 What is the short-term objective?
To secure 25% of the existing market by the end of 1978.

14 What effect would this have?
It would provide a firm basis for further expansion from 1979 onwards.

15 What other objectives does Mr Gräber refer to?
He refers to *long-term* ones.

16 What does Mr Gräber think Schweibur should do to achieve the short-term objective?
He thinks they should *offer customers leasing facilities intead of outright purchase.*

17 What is being done at the moment?
A draft leasing agreement is being drawn up by the legal department.

18 When will this be made available?
It *will be made available within the next few days.*

19 Why does Mr Gräber propose a meeting?
To discuss the report in more details and work out a sales campaign.

Key to the Exercises

Exercise A

1 We have received his *final* report.
2 *Attached* to the report you will find an appendix.
3 We have about two hundred *potential* customers for this product.
4 It will take a number of years to *achieve* our objective.
5 By 1978 we will have to increase our production *capacity*.
6 Our conclusions are *summarized* below.

draw a conclusion
set an objective
draw up a document
offer facilities
work out a campaign
meet requirements
secure sales

7   He wants you to *submit* the report by the end of the month.
8   We have overestimated the number of units we can sell, so we should *revise* our production figures.
9   I've made a number of alterations in pencil but I think these *amendments* are quite clear.
10 This product will be *available* to the public by the end of the year.
11 We should be able to sell over 1,000 units by 1979 so production will have to be *correspondingly* increased.

Exercise B

1   Our new handbook will be printed / is being printed next week.
2   No minutes were taken. / Minutes weren't taken.
3   Your dictation machine is being repaired.
4   All the market research reports on the Fonacopy are filed under 00561.
5   It was too late; the internal mail had already been collected.
6   The pencil sharpener is kept in the top left-hand drawer.
7   The complaints are being dealt with.
8   The cheque hadn't been countersigned.
    The cheque wasn't countersigned.
9   The reception will be held / is being held in the middle of next month. The exact dates won't be known till next week.
10 Mr Cayton's visit was cancelled at the last minute.
11 The canteen is closed because it is being redecorated.
12 Not me! It was typed by someone in the typing pool.

Exercise C

Mary Malone: We're very low on white copy paper. I think we *should* put in an order for some stationery. And I told Mr Heine I *would* get him some more foolscap envelopes this week.

Maureen Lynch: I'll just make a note of what we need. *Would* two packets of envelopes be enough?

Mary Malone: Oh, two *should / would* be plenty. And half a dozen boxes of copy paper.

Maureen Lynch: Now, what else *should* we order? Oh yes, we need some more carbon paper. I'll order another box.

Mary Malone: Put down two boxes, will you? One box *wouldn't* last very long.

Maureen Lynch: Is there anything else?

Key to the Exercises

Mary Malone: I always forget something. Last time I said I *would* make a list. If I did, it *would/should* certainly make things easier.

Maureen Lynch: There's only one box of paper clips in the cupboard; perhaps we *should* get some more of those?

Mary Malone: Yes, let's get a couple of boxes. That *should/would* be enough. Oh, and the typewriter ribbons, of course. We *would* be in a fix if I forgot those.

Language Laboratory Part 1: Tapescript

Drill 1

Mrs Bonheim's boss has recently been promoted. His successor, Mr Matthews, has been in the office two days, and now has a number of questions for Mrs Bonheim.

1. (Example) I don't seem to have a diary for next year yet. Didn't you order it?
It was ordered last week.

2. (Example) Ah, splendid! And when are they going to deliver it?
It'll be delivered next Wednesday.

3. (Example) Another thing; I can't find my dictation machine. Where do you keep it?
It's kept in the cupboard.

4. And haven't they delivered my filing cabinet?
It was delivered yesterday.

5. And when will they actually send it up?
It'll be sent up tomorrow morning.

6. Oh, and by the way, where do the cleaners put my typewriter?
It's brought in here every evening.

7. I'm glad to see you've had those pictures taken down.
They were taken down yesterday evening.

8. When do I get my new pictures put up?
They'll be put up tomorrow.

Drill 2

Listen to the girls in Schweibur's typing pool talking about their work.

1. (Example) Since this report is urgent I suppose we'd better type it today.
Yes, I suppose we should type it today.

2. (Example) If we had another typist, couldn't we do the work more quickly?
Yes, I suppose we would do the work more quickly.

3 If we're running out of paper I'll put in an order.
  Yes, I suppose we should put in an order.

4 If we had another cupboard we might keep things tidy.
  Yes, I suppose we would keep things tidy.

5 These papers here. Oughtn't we to file them?
  Yes, I suppose we should file them.

6 Let's ask for a new filing cabinet. Then we'd have more room.
  Yes, I suppose we would have more room.

7 Couldn't we have a copying maching? To save time, I mean.
  Yes, I suppose we would save time.

8 If you've typed those figures perhaps we'd better check them now.
  Yes, I suppose we should check them now.

Pronunciation Practice

In this unit we're going to study three more vowel sounds. Listen to the example words that are given in your book.

1 *beer*
2 *bear*
3 *bay*

Can you hear the difference between them? Which one is this?
bay

Yes, that was number three. And which one is this?
beer

That was number one. Now we're going to say ten words. Listen and decide whether the word has the vowel sound of example one, two or three, then write the number down. Are you ready? Listen carefully.

1 *fair*   6 *cheered*
2 *sheer*   7 *dared*
3 *layer*   8 *pray*
4 *mere*   9 *phase*
5 *pay*   10 *tears* (= rips)

Now here are the correct answers:

One was number two   Six was number one
Two was number one   Seven was number two
Three was number three   Eight was number three
Four was number one   Nine was number three
Five was number three   Ten was number two

Did you get most of these right? Good. Now we're going to practise the pronunciation of these vowel sounds. Look at the limerick in your book. Listen to it first.

Mister Gray loves his secretary dearly,
So one day he dictated quite clearly:
'We make a good pair,
Let us have an affair'.
Said she, 'I am yours most sincerely'.

Dialogue

Mr Heine, Schweibur's Sales Manager, is out of the office when a customer rings to complain about a delayed order. Miss Wood deals with the complaint.

Rivelini: Hallo?

Miss Wood: Mr Heine's office.

Rivelini: Can I speak to the Sales Manager, please?

Miss Wood: I'm afraid Mr Heine isn't in at the moment. Can I help you at all?

Rivelini: Yes, my name's Rivelini from IMP, Milan. I was promised delivery of 500 desk trays a week ago, and they still haven't arrived.

Miss Wood: I'm sorry to hear that, Mr Rivelini.

Rivelini: You sent an invoice, though, and I'm certainly not going to pay it until I get the goods.

Miss Wood: Naturally not, Mr Rivelini. Could you give me the invoice number?

Rivelini: PB 3856.

Miss Wood: Thank you. I'll ask Mr Heine to look into the matter as soon as I can get hold of him.

Rivelini: And please tell him we need those trays urgently.

Miss Wood: Of course. I'm very sorry there's been a delay.

Rivelini: You'll ring me back later this afternoon, then?

Miss Wood: Yes, of course, as soon as we can.

Rivelini: Right. I look forward to hearing from you. Goodbye.

Miss Wood: Goodbye, Mr Rivelini.

Correspondence

In this Key suggestions for an acceptable version are printed in bold type.

Dear Carlos,

Thank you for your letter of 10th May, in which you ask for further **information** on the Fonacopy, and some **advice on** how to promote it in Venezuela.

I apologize for not having sent you the technical **information** earlier—**it was only prepared** last week by our Information Department. I **enclose** detailed **information** on the Fonacopy, which I feel **should answer/will answer** your questions. Any points that **are not covered** by the **enclosed information** can be dealt with during the course we **are holding in** the second week in August. I think you **should** attend this course, **if** possible.

I am also sending you some guidelines on promotion of the Fonacopy, which **have** been drawn up by the Market Planning Section. I would be **grateful** if you could study these in some depth with reference to your own market, as Mr Muhammad intends to **visit** Venezuela to discuss promotion with you. **He will be writing to you very shortly on this.**

Yours sincerely

Telegrams

There has been a breakdown in the assembly line, and all orders will be delayed by two weeks.

There has been an unexpected demand for Elite typewriters. I need 100 as soon as possible. Can you supply these?

1. LORRY FORTYFIVE HIJACKED EN ROUTE ZURICH LYONS STOP CONTACT NANTUA POLICE AND REPORT

2. SINGAPORE REQUIRE ELITE TYPEWRITERS URGENT STOP REQUEST DIVERT PART YOUR ORDER STOP WILL REPLACE WITHIN TWO WEEKS STOP ANY OBJECTIONS

Language Laboratory Part 2: Tapescript

Drill 3

Miss Keller is a receptionist at Schweibur. When visitors tell her why they have come to the company or ask her advice, Miss Keller has to suggest what they should do.

1. (Example) I'd like to see Mr Gräber, but I haven't got an appointment, I'm afraid.
If you haven't got an appointment you might like to sign the visitors' book.

Language Laboratory Part 2

2 (Example) I'm interested in your range of filing cabinets.
If you're interested in our range of filing cabinets you might like to take a brochure.

3 I don't know very much about Schweibur, I'm afraid.
If you don't know very much about Schweibur you might like to have a copy of our handbook.

4 This is my first visit to Zurich.
If this is your first visit to Zurich you might like to take a map of the city.

5 I'm attending the conference.
If you're attending the conference you might like to have a programme.

6 I don't know when the flights to Rome are, I'm afraid.
If you don't know when the flights to Rome are you might like to take one of those timetables.

7 Mr Schulz asked me to wait here.
If Mr Schulz asked you to wait here you might like to take a seat for a moment.

8 I'm hoping to see a demonstration of your Fonomat switchboard.
If you're hoping to see a demonstration of our Fonomat switchboard you might like to have a word with Mr Gräber.

Drill 4

Miss Wood is a secretary in the Sales Department. People often ring her on matters that she doesn't know anything about. Sometimes nobody has told her and sometimes she has forgotten.

1 (Example) How are the preparations for the conference going?
I'm afraid I haven't heard anything about a conference. When is it taking place?

2 (Example) Don't forget to arrange for someone to show your visitor round.
I'm afraid I haven't heard anything about a visitor. When is he coming?

3 Mr Heine won't be here on the 3rd, of course, because of the sales trip.
I'm afraid I haven't heard anything about a sales trip. When is he going?

4 And could you ask Heine to see me before the reception?
I'm afraid I haven't heard anything about a reception. When is it being held?

5 He'll be back for the committee meeting though, won't he?
I'm afraid I haven't heard anything about the committee meeting. When is it taking place?

6 And we'll all be busy with the sales campaign.
I'm afraid I haven't heard anything about a sales campaign. What are we promoting?

7   You'll be at the briefing session, I suppose.
    I'm afraid I haven't heard anything about a briefing session. Who is holding it?

8   Oh, and don't forget to remind Heine about the management meeting.
    I'm afraid I haven't heard anything about a management meeting. Why is it being held now?

Active Listening

Passage 1: Mr Dudley is ringing Mr Schulz's office. Miss Miller takes the call.

Miss Miller: Mr Schulz's office, good morning.

Dudley: Ah, good morning. Dudley speaking. I'm due to meet Mr Schulz at three tomorrow afternoon.

Miss Miller: Yes, that's correct, Mr Dudley.

Dudley: Well, no-can-do, I'm afraid. I've got to take an earlier flight back to London. I'm a bit tight on time in the morning too, which makes matters more difficult. In fact, really the only time I can manage is pretty early, about 8.30. Any chance of seeing him then?

Miss Miller: I'll have to ask him when he gets back, Mr Dudley. Could you give me your telephone number and I'll call you back in about twenty minutes.

Dudley: I don't know the number, but I'm at the Grand Hotel.

Miss Miller: I'll call you at the Grand then, Mr Dudley.

Dudley: Fine. Hope Mr Schulz can make it. Goodbye.

Miss Miller: Goodbye.

What does Miss Miller have to do?
She has to ask Mr Schulz whether he can see Mr Dudley about 8.30 tomorrow morning, as Mr Dudley has to go back to London and can't manage any other time. She then has to ring Mr Dudley at the Grand and tell him whether the meeting will take place.

Passage 2: Your boss has dictated a letter onto a dictation machine.

Dear Customer,

Industrial disputes at our main factory over the last two weeks have caused, er, have unfortunately caused, er, serious loss of production, stop. Para. The dispute has now been settled but loss of production at this time of the year is most difficult to, er, recapture and this letter, er, the purpose of this letter is to advise you that our depots will be short of certain units as their locally held supplies become depleted. New paragraph. We regret the situation that has arisen for it is one which we have made great efforts to avoid, and we hope that you will, er, appreciate, er, no, we hope that you will bear with us at this most difficult time. Full stop. Yours faithfully, and that's for my signature.

Write out the letter your boss has dictated.

Role Simulation

Situation The students are asked to imagine that a visitor has arrived fifteen minutes too early for an appointment with their boss. To pass the time while he is waiting, the visitor starts up a conversation. It is the task of the secretary to respond and keep the conversation going.

Preparation The teacher should study the roles given below so that he is prepared to continue the conversation along the lines indicated.

Procedure The teacher should play the role of the visitor throughout. He should begin by introducing himself and acknowledging that he is a little early. The secretary should:
1 greet the visitor
2 say it doesn't matter about his being early and make him feel welcome
3 respond to his conversation 'openers'
4 think of another subject to talk about if the conversation seems to be flagging.

Teacher's Roles

1 I had a look round the shops this morning before I came here. My goodness, aren't things expensive? Worse than I remember them last year.

2 Well, I'll be glad to sit down for a few minutes before we start business. I've had a terrible journey out here.

3 I've been admiring your offices. Is this a new building? What do you think of these new open-plan offices?

4 Have you been working here long?

5 I was having a look at the newspaper on the way here. Isn't the news about . . . *(substitute some current event)* terrible/wonderful?

6 I believe you know a colleague of mine—Jack Ferguson. He comes here quite often.

7 Does your company have the same problem as we do in keeping their secretaries? Most of our girls just don't stay with us for very long, and we have great difficulty in replacing them.

8 Is it really true that most people here have a second weekend home in the country?

9 I've always wondered what that big building is over there/along the road/just before you get off the bus here.

10 Your English is marvellous. They must teach the language very well in the schools here.

Key to 'What is this?'

Page 65: pencil sharpener
Page 66: pencil, ball-point pen, fountain pen
Page 69: typewriter ribbon

Unit 7

Unit Summary

Introductory Recording		This episode is entitled 'A Journey'. Mr Gräber is going on a business trip next week, and Mary Malone has made the arrangements. She is discussing them with Mr Gräber, who makes one or two changes.
Text		The Text is the itinerary that Mary has finalized for Mr Gräber.
Vocabulary		There is one exercise on vocabulary within the area of overseas travel.
Structures	1	Conditional sentences: If he *takes* the 09.25 he'll *arrive* in London at 11.50. (Exercise B) He would leave at once if he could find his tickets. (Drill 1) If he had taken the 12.05 he would have arrived in London at 14.20. (Exercise B and Drill 1)
	2	Tag questions (Exercise C)
	3	*Possible/possibility* and *be able to* (Exercise D and Drill 2)
Pronunciation Practice		There is an exercise on the falling intonation in questions beginning with *who*, *what*, etc. This is followed by repetition of a limerick practising the vowel sounds [u] as in *shoe* and [ʊə] as in *sure*.
Dialogue		The situation is that of telephoning a change in the boss's travel arrangements to one of his colleagues.
Correspondence		There is a draft letter to be corrected.
Telegrams		There are four telegrams, two to be decoded, two to be encoded.
Gambits		Drill 3: Confirming *Good morning, Mr . . . I just wanted to confirm that . . . .* Drill 4: Reminding *By the way, Mr . . . , don't forget to . . . , will you?*
Active Listening		There are three passages in this unit, each one a telephone message to be written down.
Role Simulation		The students are asked to imagine that they have received a message from their boss requesting them to get information from a visitor in the building in which they are, or to pass on information to a visitor. Roles

Unit 7

Homework

are provided for the students, with the messages from the boss. The teacher should take the role of the visitor.

The written gambit introduced in this unit is:

Clearing up misunderstandings.

Introductory recording

Tapescript

A Journey
Mary Malone's boss, Erich Gräber, is going on a business trip next week. Mary has made most of the arrangements, and she knows Mr Gräber will want to discuss them with her.

Malone: Yes, Mr Gräber?

Gräber: Er, look, Mary, I'd just like to run over the details of my trip next week. If you could just bring in the itinerary, and so on, yes?

Malone: Yes, Mr Gräber, right away.

Gräber: Good. Now, I'd like to get this over fairly quickly, if we could. I've got this meeting to go to, haven't I, on salary increases?

Malone. Oh, yes; do you think there's a possibility of an increase for me?

Gräber: Well, I wouldn't like to commit myself, of course, but I think it is not likely we would be discussing your case if there wasn't quite a possibility, would we? Erm, now, could you run through the itinerary you've prepared and I'll ask any questions that may come up, shall I? You're going to check the details with the Travel Section, aren't you, to finalize them?

Malone: Oh, yes, with Miss Schmidt.

Gräber: Good, good.

Malone: You start on, erm, Monday. Fly to Dublin on, er, BA 318. You have to check in at 08.15 and . . .

Gräber: 08.15? Good heavens, there's surely a slightly later flight, isn't there?

Malone: Well, yes, there is one, but it wouldn't give you very long in Dublin. Don't forget you're flying back to London the same evening.

Gräber: Oh, yes, of course. Ah well, just have to get up early, won't I? Now . . .

Malone: I'm afraid you will. Yes. You arrive in Dublin at 12.55. You're met by Mr Daly and you have lunch.

Gräber: Erm, will I be able to spend any time seeing the city, d'you think?

Malone: Well, I'm not too sure about that really. It rather depends. The meeting starts at 13.30. If it finishes before four there may be time for a quick tour . . .

Gräber: Then I'll have to see if it's possible to keep the meeting short. So then . . . ?

Malone: Then Mr Daly'll put you on the London plane. That's BA 168, which last time you took it . . .

Gräber: Ah, yes, I remember, that's the one that was so late last time, yes? Isn't it? OK. Now, where'm I staying in London?

Malone: You're booked into the Caravel, quite near the airport.

Gräber: Caravel? Wasn't it possible to get me into the Parkway as usual?

Malone. Well, the Parkway would have involved much more travelling for you, Mr Gräber, because the firm you're visiting is located in Hounslow, quite near the airport. You'll be able to . . .

Gräber: Oh, I see. Yes. Fine, then. Erm, you have the hotel telephone number, do you?

Malone: Well, no, I haven't. But I'll be able to get it from the Travel Section for you.

Gräber: Well, if you could, hm? There are one or two friends I've got in London that I'd like to invite. For a drink or a meal or something. So . . .

Malone: Yes, I'll ask them for that, Mr Gräber . . . *(Fade)*

Malone: . . . and he asked me to get the Caravel telephone number. Have you got it?

Schmidt: Er, would you hold on a moment? Yes, here it is. 01-573 6842.

Malone: 6842. Now then, there was something else. Oh, yes, is it possible to change the hotel in Copenhagen? He's been booked into the Tivoli, hasn't he? He says he's already stayed there twice and found it rather depressing.

Schmidt: Well, I suppose it might be possible to change it. It would have been a lot easier if we'd known earlier, of course. But we'll do our best, naturally.

Malone: Oh, thank you very much. And another thing. A change in the Helsinki—Paris flight. I did look it up, but I just wanted to confirm that there is a flight leaving earlier . . .

Schmidt: Earlier? Are you sure? I mean, Mr Gräber is well known for not liking early starts, isn't he?

Malone: Yes, well, I appreciate that, but, erm, you see, Mr Gräber's supposed to be meeting his wife in Paris. And since her plane arrives quite early . . .

Schmidt: Oh, yes, now I understand. Well, it would have helped if we had had this information last week. But I think we'll be able to make the change. Yes. Now, erm, let's see. Er, yes, the new time . . . the new departure time would be 08.45 and that would arrive in Paris 12.35. Yes, that's right.

Malone: Yes, that's what I thought. Good. Thank you very much, Miss Schmidt. Now, was there anything else? Oh, yes, the hotel room in Paris. That could be changed from a single to a double, couldn't it?

Schmidt: Oh, yes, I should think so. That won't be difficult. Erm, I'll do that today. Now. Any other points?

Malone: I don't think so, no. Let me just think a little. Er, oh, the tickets . . . Mr Gräber won't be in the office on Monday . . .

Schmidt: Oh, yes. If the changes are made today we'll be able to send them up before we close today. That's all in order now, isn't it?

Malone: Oh, yes, that's fine. Thank you very much indeed, Miss Schmidt. Goodbye now.

Schmidt: Goodbye, Miss Malone.

Comprehension Questions

1. What are Mary and Mr Gräber discussing?
   Mr Gräber's trip next week.

2. Is Mary going to get a salary increase?
   Mr Gräber doesn't say, although there's a possibility that she will.

3. Where is Mr Gräber going first?
   Dublin.

4. What does Mr Gräber want to do in addition to the meeting with Mr Daly?
   He wants to see something of the city.

5. Where is he going after that?
   London.

6. Was he happy with the hotel Mary had booked him into?
   No, he wasn't.

7. Did he accept Mary's reservation?
   Yes, he did.

8. Who did Mary confirm the arrangements with after she had gone over with Mr Gräber?
   With Miss Schmidt in the Travel Section.

9. Did Miss Schmidt welcome the changes Mary wanted to make?
   No, it would have been easier if she had been told earlier.

10. Could she make the changes?
    Yes.

11 Who is Mr Gräber meeting in Paris?
His wife.

Text: A Journey

Comprehension Questions

The words and phrases in italics are quoted verbatim from the Text.

1 What is an itinerary?
A detailed plan of a journey.

2 Which towns is Mr Gräber going to visit?
Dublin, London, Copenhagen, Helsinki and *Paris*.

3 How will he travel to Dublin?
By plane. (By air.)

4 What will Mr Gräber have to do at the air terminal before he gets on the bus to the airport?
He'll have to *check in*.

5 What time will he have to check in? (What's another way of saying that?)
Eight fifteen; eight fifteen am; quarter past eight in the morning.

6 What will happen when he arrives in Dublin?
Mr Daly will pick him up at the airport and take him to lunch.

7 What will he be doing that afternoon?
He'll be attending a *meeting at Schweibur*.

8 Will Mr Gräber have any time for sightseeing in Dublin?
No, he probably won't. He has to leave for *London* at *16.50*.

9 What kind of accommodation has Mr Gräber got in London?
He's got a *single room with shower* at the *Caravel Hotel*.

10 Why is Mr Gräber going to London?
He's got a meeting with *Mr Jarrow* of *Spears and Wilcox* on the following day.

11 What is his next appointment?
He's having *lunch* with *Mr Hughes* at the *Cafe Royal*.

12 Has accommodation in Copenhagen been arranged for him?
Yes, a *single room with bath* has been *booked* at the *Skagerrak Hotel*.

13 Will Mr Gräber have time to see anything in Copenhagen?
Yes, he'll have the evening free.

14 Who is he going to see the following morning?
He's going to see *Mr Nording* of *Andersen's*.

15 What does AY 804 stand for?
It's his flight number to Helsinki.

	16	Why hasn't a hotel been booked in Helsinki?
		Because Mr Gräber is going to *stay with Mr Valkama*.
	17	Who is Mr Valkama?
		He's a member of staff of *Schweibur's* branch in *Finland*.
	18	How long will Mr Gräber spend at Schweibur's Finnish branch?
		The whole day.
	19	Can Mr Gräber fly direct to Paris the next day?
		No, he can't. He has to transfer to another flight (airline) in *Stockholm*.

Key to the Exercises

Exercise A	1	A detailed plan of a journey is called an *itinerary*.
	2	Most companies buy tickets through a *travel agent/agency*.
	3	I've got your foreign *currency* and *travellers* cheques.
	4	I've already *booked* the hotel rooms for him.
	5	Mr Shermann doesn't know what flight he's coming back on, so he's got an *open* ticket.
	6	He doesn't like travelling by train, so he's *hiring* a car at the airport.
	7	The *flight number* is BA 168.
	8	You have to *check in* an hour before departure.
	9	I'm not going on holiday. It's a *business trip*.
	10	No, not first class, *tourist* class, please.

Exercise B	1	If he had taken the 1205 he would have arrived in London at 1420.
	2	If he had taken the 1415 he would have arrived in London at 1805.
	3	If he had taken the 1900 he would have arrived in London at 2115.
	4	If he had taken the 2000 he would have arrived in London at 0245.
	5	If he had taken the 1205 he would have had to transfer.
	6	If he had taken the 1415 he would have had to transfer at Copenhagen.
	7	If he had taken the 1900 he wouldn't have had to transfer.
	8	If he had taken the 2000 he would have had to transfer at Copenhagen.

	1	If he takes the 0925 he'll arrive in London at 1150.
	2	If he takes the 1205 he'll arrive in London at 1555.
	3	If he takes the 1530 he'll arrive in London at 1745.
	4	If he takes the 1815 he'll arrive in London at 2030.
	5	If he takes the 2025 he'll arrive in London at 0245.
	6	If he takes the 0925 he won't have to transfer.
	7	If he takes the 1205 he'll have to transfer at Copenhagen.
	8	If he takes the 1530 he won't have to transfer.
	9	If he takes the 1815 he won't have to transfer.
	10	If he takes the 2025 he'll have to transfer at Copenhagen.

Exercise C	1	Mr Gräber has signed the letters, hasn't he?
	2	You didn't leave the petty cash out, did you?

Key to the Exercises

3 The post is in the out-tray, isn't it?
4 You have put the cover on the adding machine, haven't you?
5 The windows aren't open, are they?
6 You did put the files away, didn't you?
7 The photocopier isn't still switched on, is it?
8 You will lock the door behind you, won't you?
9 You have typed the minutes, haven't you?
10 Mr Gräber did postpone the meeting tomorrow, didn't he?

Exercise D

1 Will you be able to come on July 15th?
2 I was wondering if it was possible to postpone the meeting.
3 We are able to deliver according to schedule.
4 We are able to supply the parts you require.
5 Will you be able to let me know next week?
6 It is possible to replace the sub-component you mention by . . .
7 We were able to meet Mr Schumann at the exhibition.
8 It is possible to replace faulty units immediately.
9 Is it possible to meet in London on 15th June?
10 I was able to locate the fault within two hours.

Language Laboratory Part 1: Tapescript

Drill 1

Listen to these two secretaries in the Travel Department.

1 (Example) Mr Gräber ought to leave at once.
   He would leave at once if he could find his tickets.

2 (Example) I really think we should take on more staff.
   We would take on more staff if there were any available.

3 Mr Schranz looks awful. He ought to take a holiday.
   He would take a holiday if he had time.

4 The Grand Hotel wants to attract more customers.
   It would attract more customers if it made them feel more welcome.

5 Miss Schmidt might do the accounts tomorrow.
   She would do them if she had a moment to herself.

Now listen carefully again, please.

6 (Example) Mr Fromm forgot his passport.
   He wouldn't have forgotten it if he hadn't been in such a hurry.

7 (Example) Mr Gräber and Mr Heine caught the afternoon flight.
   They wouldn't have caught it if they hadn't missed the morning one.

8 Mr Shermann has cancelled the meeting.
   He wouldn't have cancelled it if Miss Lachenal hadn't been called away.

9   Our French visitors were late this morning.
    They wouldn't have been late if they hadn't decided to stay outside the town.

10 Mr Standop has gone to Spain.
    He wouldn't have gone to Spain if the Personnel Manager hadn't insisted on it.

Drill 2

When Mary Malone falls ill a few days before a sales conference, the office is thrown into confusion. Mr Gräber and Mr Donovan, of the Dublin branch, are wondering how they are going to manage.

1   (Example)   Miss Miller types pretty fast. Can she type the report before five?
    No, I'm afraid she won't be able to type it before five.

2   (Example)   And the sales conference is on Thursday. Can it be postponed?
    No, I'm afraid it won't be possible to postpone it.

3   How good is Mrs Schaller's English? Can she write the minutes?
    No, I'm afraid she won't be able to write them.

4   Well, can't Miss Miller translate them?
    No, I'm afraid she won't be able to translate them.

5   Do you think the agenda can be circulated today?
    No, I'm afraid it won't be possible to circulate it today.

6   Look at these figures in the report. I wonder if the salesmen can understand them.
    No, I'm afraid they won't be able to undestand them.

7   Is the new conference room ready? Can it be used yet?
    No, I'm afraid it won't be possible to use it.

8   Miss Keller asks if she can have some time off on Tuesday.
    No, I'm afraid she won't be able to have any time off on Tuesday.

Pronunciation Practice

In this unit we're going to study one of the intonation patterns of English. Intonation is the way your voice goes up and down when you speak. Listen to these questions.

Who was there?   *When is that?*
Which is best?   *Where is Karl?*
What was said?   *Who will go?*

Now, all those questions began with a question word like *who* or *where*. Did you notice that the speaker's voice went down on the last word? Listen again.

Who was there?

Did you also notice that the first word and the last word were much longer and louder than the middle word? The middle word was very short and quick. Now repeat these questions. We will only give you enough time to say the question at the correct speed. Remember to make your voice go down on the last word. Listen and repeat.

Who was there? *When is that?*
Which is best? *Where is Karl?*
What was said? *Who will go?*

Now listen to these questions.

What's the time? *Who've you seen?*
Where's the file? *How's your wife?*
What's his name? *Who'll be there?*

These questions have an extra word in them but that word is shortened to apostrophe -s or apostrophe -ve. You must still say the question in the same amount of time as before. Don't forget to make your voice fall on last word. Listen and repeat these questions.

What's the time? *Who've you seen?*
Where's the file? *How's your wife?*
What's his name? *Who'll be there?*

Now we have another limerick for you to practise your pronunciation. But this time we want you to pay more attention to the short quick syllables. Listen to the limerick first. Listen very carefully to the vowel sounds in the words that are not printed in capital letters.

The firemen were full of assurance,
But the heat was past human endurance.
There was nought they could do
It was burnt through and through,
Thank God we renewed the insurance.

Dialogue

Mr Konstanz is in Geneva today. Before he left he asked his secretary, Miss Miller, to telephone Mr Hernandez, a colleague of his in Madrid. Miss Miller is to inform Mr Hernandez that Mr Konstanz has had to alter his travel arangements for his trip to Spain next week.

Hernandez: Hernandez speaking.

Miss Miller: Good afternoon, Mr Hernandez. This is Mr Konstanz's secretary from Schweibur Headquarters.

Hernandez: Good afternoon. Miss Miller, isn't it? What can I do for you?

Miss Miller: Mr Konstanz asked me to tell you he's had to make some changes in his travel arrangements.

Hernandez: I see.

Miss Miller: He won't be coming on Thursday, but on Wednesday, if that's alright with you.

Hernandez: I should think that would be OK. What time's he arriving?

Miss Miller: He'll be arriving at the airport at 12.10 by Swissair flight 585.

Hernandez: Good. I'll have a car pick him up. Would you like me to tell his hotel he'll be a day early?

Miss Miller: That would be very kind of you, thank you. It's the Majestic.

Hernandez: One thing. When will he be leaving now?

Miss Miller: He'll be leaving as originally planned, on the Friday.

Hernandez: That's fine. Well, thank you for letting me know.

Miss Miller: Not at all, Mr Hernandez, and thank you for your help.

Hernandez: Not at all. Goodbye.

Miss Miller: Goodbye.

Correspondence

In this Key suggestions for an acceptable version are printed in bold type.

Dear Mr Cardenali,

Thank you for your letter of 15th July **concerning / regarding** your visit to Zurich. **Unfortunately** I have *(omit)* to visit Geneva **next Tuesday / on the Tuesday of next week** and so **it won't be possible for me / I won't be able** to see you then. **Is there any chance of your coming / Could you come** on Wednesday? If you could, I would be delighted to meet you again.

We are having a slight problem with your **accommodation. There are so many tourists here / Zurich is so busy** at this time of the year, *(omit)* I wonder if therefore you would have **any** objection to staying **with us on** the Tuesday and Wednesday nights—**I shall be** back from Geneva at 16.00 **on** the Tuesday. **My wife and I** would be only too pleased **to put** you up.

I'd be grateful if you would / Could you please ring my secretary and let her know whether Wednesday is convenient **for** you?

I look forward to seeing you again.

Yours,

Telegrams

Benzalotti are not prepared to do business with us unless they get 5 ½ %

Telegrams

discount on the goods they buy. Would you please let me know whether I should go any further with negotiations?

Martinez says that the goods we sent them were faulty. I have promised to have these replaced free of charge. Please inform Martinez when the replacements will be delivered to Seville.

1 BENZALOTTI RUMOURED SWITCHING IOE STOP INVESTIGATE AND INFORM STOP

2 AZIZ IN ZURICH DAY AFTER YOUR DEPARTURE STOP TRY ARRANGE EXTRA DAY TO MEET STOP

Language Laboratory Part 2: Tapescript

Drill 3

Miss Jones is secretary to Mr Shermann at Schweibur. She often has to confirm arrangements over the phone.

1 (Example)   Santos speaking.
Good morning Mr Santos. I just wanted to confirm that you are coming to see Mr Shermann next week.

2 (Example 2)   International Travel Agency, good morning.
Good morning. I just wanted to confirm that you have posted Mr Shermann's tickets to Spain.

3 Darcy here.
Good morning Mr Darcy. I just wanted to confirm that you are expecting Mr Shermann next Friday.

4 Grand Hotel, good morning.
Good morning. I just wanted to confirm that you have reserved a table for six for Mr Shermann tonight.

5 Lampwick, good morning.
Good morning Mr Lampwick. I just wanted to confirm that you have received our invoice number 5541.

6 Kraus.
Good morning Mr Kraus. I just wanted to confirm that you are coming to Zurich on Tuesday.

7 Harkwood's Transport, can I help you?
Good morning. I just wanted to confirm that you have sent off our consignment number 3388 to the docks.

8 Masters speaking.
Good morning Mr Masters. I just wanted to confirm that you have received our telegram of yesterday.

Drill 4

Schweibur executives often ask their secretaries to remind them about things they might otherwise forget.

1. (Example) *By the way, Mr Gräber, don't forget to ring Mr Karlberger, will you?*
2. (Example) *By the way, Mr Konstanz, don't forget to dictate a letter to Frankfurt, will you?*
3. *By the way, Mr Schulz, don't forget to have a word with Mr Braun, will you?*
4. *By the way, Mr Flügel, don't forget to sign your letters, will you?*
5. *By the way, Miss Lachenal, don't forget to contact Mr Steuermann, will you?*
6. *By the way, Mr Heine, Don't forget to read the sales contract through, will you?*
7. *By the way, Mr Hoffman, don't forget to ring Mr Pellegrini, will you?*
8. *By the way, Mr Müller, don't forget to have a look at the quarterly report, will you?*

Active Listening

Listen to this telephone conversation. Mr Heine, Betty Wood's boss, is visiting a Mr Deferre in Brussels. Miss Wood suddenly receives this telephone message.

Miss Wood: Mr Heine's office, good morning.

Deferre: Good morning. Deferre here, from Brussels. Your boss asked me tell you he's not going straight back to Zurich today, but he is going via Frankfurt, and spending the night there. Could you phone his wife and let her know?

Miss Wood: Yes, of course.

Deferre: Now, he's hoping to get on BA 784, reaching Zurich at 18.25 tomorrow. Could you arrange for a taxi to meet him?

Miss Wood: Yes, certainly, Mr Deferre.

Deferre: He'll let you know any further changes in plan from Frankfurt, OK?

Miss Wood: Yes, fine.

Deferre: Goodbye, then.

Miss Wood: Goodbye, Mr Deferre, and thank you.

What is the message Miss Wood should give Mrs Heine?
Mr Heine is not coming straight back to Zurich, but going to Frankfurt, where he'll be spending the night. He's hoping to get on BA 784

reaching Zurich at 18.25 tomorrow. He'll telephone the office if there are any other changes in plan.

Passage 2: Miss Miller's boss hadn't arrived at the office when she received the following telephone message for him.

Miss Miller: Mr Konstanz's office.

Hernandez: Good morning. My name is Hernandez. Can I speak to Mr Konstanz, please?

Miss Miller: I'm afraid Mr Konstanz isn't in yet, Mr Hernandez. Can I take a message?

Hernandez: Yes, could you? I was to see Mr Konstanz this afternoon, but it now seems extremely unlikely that I shall be able to make it. Apparently somebody tried to hijack an aeroplane here at Madrid and the place has been temporarily closed. Now, I may be able to get a later flight arriving in Zurich this evening, in which case I would hope to see Mr Konstanz some time tomorrow. If I can't get a flight today I'll ring again either this afternoon or at, say, ten o'clock tomorrow morning. Have you got that?

Miss Miller: Yes, thank you. I'll get that message to Mr Konstanz as soon as possible.

What is the message Miss Miller should give her boss?
Mr Hernandez is unlikely to arrive this afternoon, because of an attempted hijack at Madrid, which has temporarily closed the airport. He hopes to arrive this evening, and see Mr Konstanz tomorrow. If he can't get a flight today, he'll ring either later or at ten tomorrow morning.

Passage 3: Miss Jones has to deal with a telephone call for her boss, Mr Shermann.

Miss Jones: Mr Shermann's office.

Kollberg: Good morning. Kollberg here from Andersson's in Gothenburg. I wonder if I could leave a message for Mr Shermann. It's about your next shipment of pinewood. I'm afraid we can't supply this straight away but in view of the urgency of your order, I've been on to our Norwegian subsidiary in Narvik. They say they can meet your order and will ship the wood on Friday from there. OK?

Miss Jones: Yes, I'll let Mr Shermann know as soon as he's in, Mr Kollberg. And thank you very much.

What is the message Miss Jones should give Mr Shermann?
Mr Kollberg of Andersson's, Gothenburg, says he can't supply our urgent order for pinewood straightaway, but is shipping it from Narvik through their Norwegian subsidiary on Friday.

Role Simulation

Situation The students are asked to imagine that they have received a message from their boss requesting them to get information from or relay information to a visitor in the building.

Preparation The teacher should study the messages given below and draw up his own role for the part of the visitor.

Procedure The teacher should play the role of the visitor throughout. Each student should be given one of the roles which contains a message from their boss. They should begin by:

1 apologizing for the interruption or requesting a few words with the visitor
2 getting or relaying the information as indicated in the roles.

Messages

1 I'm going to be slightly delayed for my appointment with Mr Patel—I'm still waiting for a copy of the contract in the Legal Department. Make my apologies and look after him till I get there. I'm supposed to be taking him out to lunch afterwards. I don't know whether I can take him to the canteen or not—you know the diet restrictions some of these Indians have. Find out what sort of things he can eat and drink.

2 *Telephone Message:* Your boss phoned to say that he's been delayed in town. Could you catch Mr Lopez before he goes into his meeting with Mr Lunden and ask him if he could meet your boss in town instead—in the bar of the Imperial Hotel. Apologize for the change in plan. Find out if this is OK by him, give him directions how to get there and find out what time he'll be finished with Mr Lunden so that you can confirm with your boss.

3 Can you get hold of Mr Gregory from our English subsidiary (he should be with Andersson). Ask him if he'd be kind enough to take back a parcel to Brentwood for me to give to Tony. Warn him that it's rather heavy and offer to refund any excess baggage. If it's OK by him, find out where he'll be tonight so that I can deliver the parcel.

4 Can you find Mr Lebrun? I think he must have gone off with the wrong folder after the meeting we had this morning. See if this brown folder belongs to him and see if he's got a brown folder of mine, unmarked, with sales reports of the GX range in it.

5 I can't find the file on the development of the TT range. I know Hoffman from our German subsidiary was working with it. Could you go to his office and find out if he's got it, or if he knows what happened to it. It's certainly not in the filing cabinet—I've looked.

6 Please find Mr Lawrence, the American visitor who was here earlier on.

I'll probably want to get in touch with him in the next two or three days. I know he's leaving tonight and is going to Canada. Find out his movements over the next couple of days and ask him where I can contact him.

7   I forgot to get the expenses claim from that young man who was in for an interview just now—van Galen, the Dutchman. Could you chase after him and get all the details of his expenses from him?

8   I've just heard that our biggest Greek customer has decided to stop doing business with us. I'm expecting Mouskouris, our agent in Greece, to call in at the office tomorrow. Explain that I have to go to this meetings and say I'm sorry not to be able to see him. Find out from him why we've lost this customer.

9   Had lunch with a Mr O'Shea today. He mentioned something about a survey his company had done of new developments in production techniques. I'd be interested in reading it. Could you ask him for the full reference and find out if I can get hold of a copy?

10 I've got to arrange a programme for the Managing Director of our Portuguese subsidiary. I know their Sales Manager, a Mr Pereira, is here at the moment. Could you get hold of him and find out what his MD would be most interested in doing, and who he'd like to speak to.

Key to 'What is this?'

Page 77: ashtray and cigarette
Page 78: calendar
Page 82: lighter
Page 83: elastic bands

Unit 8

Unit Summary

Introductory Recording	This episode is entitled 'Arriving for a Meeting'. Mary Malone has been asked to welcome some visitors and talk to them while they are waiting to go into a meeting.
Text	The Text is the minutes of the meeting which the visitors attended.
Vocabulary	Exercise A is a three-part exercise on vocabulary which appears in the Text.
Structures	1 Indirect speech. (Exercise B and Drill 1) Mr Gräber *suggested that* ... 2 Gerund/Infinitive. (Exercise C and Drill 2) It wouldn't be *advisable to* ... There wouldn't be much *sense in* ... *ing* ...
Pronunciation Practice	This deals with the difference between using a rising and a falling intonation on questions beginning with interrogatives. This is followed by repetition of a limerick practising the vowel sounds [aɪ] as in *white*, [aɪə] as in *higher* and [aʊ] as in *out*.
Dialogue	The situation is that of a secretary making a complaint to a hotel.
Correspondence	There is a draft letter to be corrected.
Telegrams	There are four telegrams, two to be decoded and two to be encoded.
Gambits	Drill 3: Redirecting a call *I'm afraid this office doesn't deal with the ... of ..., but if you'll hold the line I'll put you through to the ... department.* Drill 4: Passing of information *Yes, Mr Heine asked me to tell you ...*
Active Listening	There are four passages in this unit. 1 A telephone message 2 A recorded instruction 3 A recorded instruction 4 A recorded instruction
Role Simulation	The students are asked to imagine that there is a visitor in their office.

Unit Summary   121

They have to make helpful suggestions or offer assistance to the visitor if he needs it. Roles are provided for the teacher, who plays the part of the visitor throughout.

Homework

The written gambit introduced in this unit deals with:

Stalling

Introductory Recording

Tapescript

Arriving for a Meeting

This morning Mr Gräber has a meeting with four quality supervisors from different companies within the Schweibur group. He has asked Mary Malone to bring them into his office when they have all arrived. So Mary is in her office this morning, waiting for the first one to arrive.

Achebe: Er, excuse me.

Malone: Oh, good morning, can I help you?

Achebe: Oh yes. My name is Ikeocha Achebe.

Malone: Yes, Mr Achebe. For the meeting, isn't it? Yes, Mr Gräber is expecting you. Erm, I think we've met before . . .

Achebe: Oh yes, we have. I'm a bit surprised you remember. You're Miss Malone, aren't you?

Malone: Yes, that's right. And it was at the fiftieth anniversary here, wasn't it?

Achebe: Oh yes. A few months ago, in fact.

Malone: Yes. And since then . . . ?

Achebe: Oh, you know, I've been on a training course here, since we met that time. Quality supervision. It's almost over, in fact.

Malone: Oh, then I expect you're looking forward to going home.

Achebe: Well, I am really, yes, though I've got quite used to living and working here in Zurich, you know.

Malone: Oh, that's good. Anyway, will you take a seat? Mr Gräber has asked you all to wait until . . .

Achebe: Oh thank you, yes.

Malone: Excuse me just a moment, please.

Malone: Mr Gräber's office. Who's calling, please?

Hertz: Hertz, Bern. It's about the GL3 contract. I . . .

Malone: Contract? GL3?

Hertz: Yes, contract. You know what that is? I . . .

Malone: I'm sorry, Mr Hertz, I think you've got the wrong extension. If you'll hold on, I'll transfer you . . .

Hertz: Yes, all right, but don't get me cut off. This is the third time . . .

Malone: I've no intention of getting you cut off. Hold on, please.

Malone: Oh, switchboard. Will you transfer Mr Hertz's call to the contract section? Oh, and he's worried about being cut off. Thank you.

Fox: Earl Fox. For the meeting. Erich in?

Malone: Oh, yes, Mr Fox. Erm, Mr Gräber thought he would prefer you all to go in together. So we're just waiting for the others. Have you met Mr Achebe? From the Lagos branch?

Fox: Oh, hi.

Achebe: Hello Mr Fox.

Malone: Hallo, Therese. How are you?

Lachenal: Very well, indeed, Mary. And you?

Malone: Fine, thanks. Would you like to have a seat? We're just waiting for Mr . . . , erm, Aguirre to arrive. Do you know, er, . . .

Lachenal: Mr Achebe? Yes, of course. He was with me on part of his training course here.

Achebe: Nice to see you again, Therese.

Lachenal: And you, Ikeocha. You succeeded in finding your way here all right? That's good.

Malone: And have you met Mr Fox? Miss Lachenal, of the Zurich factory.

Lachenal: No, I haven't. How do you do?

Fox: Oh, hi. Glad to meet you. Say, I really think there's a good case for holding these meetings more often, don't you? You know, meeting people in the same work . . .

Malone: Well, I think Mr Gräber realizes the benefits of getting together like this, but of course, the expense . . .

Fox: Well, Schweibur haven't paid out on me today. I'm over here on holiday. Doing Europe. Just stopped off for this meeting.

Fox: Hey, Edmundo, how are you? We were beginning to think you weren't coming. You people know Edmund Aguirre?

Aguirre: I'm really sorry I'm so late. I do apologize. How are you, Earl? Good to see you again.

Introductory Recording

Fox: Good to see you, buddy.

Aguirre: How's Vancouver?

Fox: I think it's still there. Haven't seen it for a month. I'm on tour, all round Europe.

Malone: Aherm. Mr Aguirre, I'd like to introduce Mr Achebe.

Achebe: How do you do?

Malone: From our Lagos branch.

Aguirre: Very pleased to meet you.

Malone: And this is Miss Lachenal. She's with us here in Zurich, of course.

Aguirre: Yes, yes. Delighted to meet you. Nice to meet you all. I tell you what. There's no chance to talk now, we've got this meeting. But what about some lunch afterwards? I know a very good place . . .

Fox: Well, you'll have to count me out. I thought this would be a good opportunity to go and see Lake Constance. So I'll be going right after the meeting.

Aguirre: Fine, Earl. But do you two object to eating with me?

Chorus: No, we'd like to. Thank you.

Aguirre: Oh, that's fine, then.

Malone: Er, Mr Aguire. Ready now?

Aguirre: Yes, of course. Please.

Malone: Everyone's here now, Mr Gräber. I'll bring them in, shall I?

Gräber: Thank you, Mary. Yes, bring them in. And you'll come too, yes? I think I told you there would be notes to be taken . . .

Malone: Yes, you did. We'll be right in.

Comprehension Questions

1. When did Mr Achebe and Mary Malone meet before?
   At Schweibur's fiftieth anniversary.

2. What has Mr Achebe been doing since then?
   He's been on a training course (on quality supervision) at Headquarters.

3. While Mary is talking to Mr Achebe the phone rings. What does she do with this call?
   She transfers it (to the contract section).

4. Why doesn't Mary show Mr Fox and Mr Achebe into Mr Gräber's office?
   Mr Gräber wants them all to go in together so they are waiting for the others to arrive.

5   After Mary has greeted Mr Fox what does she do out of politeness?
    She introduces him to Mr Achebe.

6   Does the next visitor, Miss Lachenal, know both men?
    She knows Mr Achebe but she doesn't know Mr Fox.

7   Has Mr Fox come all the way from Canada specially for this meeting?
    No, he's in Zurich on holiday.

8   How well do Mr Fox and Mr Aguirre know each other?
    They're old friends.

9   What does Mr Aguirre suggest that they do after the meeting?
    He suggests they have lunch together.

10 Do they all agree to this?
    No, Mr Fox has to go straight after the meeting (to see Lake Constance).

11 Why does Mary go into the meeting with the four visitors?
    To take notes from Mr Gräber.

Text: Minutes

Comprehension Questions

The words and phrases in italics are quoted verbatim from the Text.

1   What are these the minutes of?
    (Of) *a meeting*.

2   Where did the meeting take place?
    It was *held at Schweibur Headquarters*.

3   Which company does Mr Fox work for?
    Offekwip Inc, Vancouver.

4   Who apologized?
    Mr Gräber.

5   What did he apologize for?
    The absence of the production manager.

6   Was the production manager expected to be at the meeting?
    Yes, but *he was unable to attend*.

7   What did Mr Gräber think needed improving?
    Quality supervision methods.

8   Are Schweibur products inspected at the factories?
    Yes, *regularly*.

9   Who had to apologize to customers?
    Marketing staff.

10 How often did they have to do this?
    Rather frequently.

11 What did this suggest?
    Inefficient inspection methods by the supervisors.

12 What did Mr Gräber think they should consider?
    Setting up some research (into these inspection methods).

13 What was the first reason Mr Gräber gave for the urgent need to reduce poor quality?
    Several important sales campaigns were about to be launched.

14 Who does he hope will place large orders?
    Trade delegations visiting Switzerland in the near future.

15 What took place after Mr Gräber's talk?
    A *discussion.*

16 What was Mr Aguirre's opinion on research into this problem of poor quality supervision?
    That it *could be very beneficial.*

17 What did Mr Aguirre think the majority of supervisors should be?
    More *flexible (in their methods).*

18 According to Mr Fox, why were many inspection staff rather conservative?
    Because they tended to be older employees.

19 What did Miss Lachenal think of Mr Fox's opinion?
    She agreed that it *was probably correct.*

20 What did the detailed discussion concern?
    Some aspects of the problem that might be examined by the research team.

21 Who else would be involved in the arrangements to be made by Mr Gräber?
    The Production Department.

22 Who had taken a training course at Headquarters?
    Mr Achebe.

23 What was to be circulated?
    His *report.*

24 What sort of trip was Mr Gräber going to make?
    A trip round the world.

25 What was the purpose of his trip?
    To visit *many Schweibur associate and subsidiary companies.*

Key to the Exercises

Exercise A   1   There were only about half a dozen people at the monthly departmental *meeting.*

2 The maintenance engineer *inspected* the machine very carefully but could find nothing wrong with it.
3 The quality of the food in the restaurant she recommended was rather *poor*.
4 We asked the manager for his opinion and we think that it is probably the *correct* one.
5 The work of quality supervisors is with factory products, which they inspect *regularly*.
6 The Board has decided to look into this problem at once, and a *research* team will be appointed very soon.
7 'We should all look out for new techniques to try out, and generally be more *flexible* in our working methods.'—The Chairman.

quality supervisors;
production staff; production supervisors; production managers; production methods;
inspection staff; inspection supervisors; inspection managers; inspection methods;
marketing staff; marketing campaigns: marketing managers; marketing methods;
sales staff; sales campaigns; sales managers;

Exercise B

These are possible answers. There are other acceptable alternatives.

Mr Flügel *explained* that profits *had* dropped recently owing to the high rate of inflation. He *pointed out* that the Purchasing Department *was* now having to pay double for supplies of raw materials.

Mr Gräber *asked* if *they could* cut down any of *their* costs.

Mr Heine *thought* transport costs *seemed* very high.

Mr Boileau *explained* that this *was* due to the increased charges for air-freighting goods.

Mr Heine *suggested* that *they should* ship *their* goods down the Rhine from Basel. He *felt* that would reduce costs considerably.

Mr Shermann *pointed out* that if *they did* that, they *would* have to revise all *their* schedules to allow for the longer time it would take.

Mr Boileau *agreed* that *they* would have time to despatch goods well in advance to make sure the customers got them on time.

Mr Gräber *wondered* if there *wasn't* a risk of delays. He *felt* the volume of traffic on the Rhine *is/was* very heavy.

Mr Heine *believed* that delays would certainly be very bad for public relations. He *felt* they *couldn't* afford to lose customers through delayed deliveries.

Key to the Exercises 127

Mr Flügel *wondered whether* they *weren't* perhaps trying to cut expenses in the wrong areas. He *thought* it *made* more sense to economize on some of the non-essential expenditure. He *suggested* that they *take* a closer look at some of *their* R & D programmes.

Exercise C

1 It would be inadvisable *to* increase the standard departmental petty cash float.
2 It would be a good idea *to* train more girls as audio-typists.
3 There would be no sense *in* chang*ing* the company letterheads.
4 It wouldn't be practical *to* work flexible hours.
5 We can see the benefits *of* hav*ing* lectures on safety in the factory.
6 We can see some purpose *in* elect*ing* a committee to deal with staff-management relations.
7 It would be perfectly possible *to* start up a sports club.
8 There would be no difficulty *in* keep*ing* the canteen open till 5.30.
9 We appreciate the advantages *of* hav*ing* more inter-departmental meetings.
10 There would be a good case *for* improv*ing* the pension scheme.

Language Laboratory Part 1: Tapescript

Drill 1

A trade delegation from Japan is visiting Schweibur in three weeks' time. Two secretaries are discussing the arrangements. Unfortunately they have both heard different stories about these arrangements.

1 (Example) Miss Wood is in charge of the arrangements, I believe.
Really? I understood Miss Malone was in charge of the arrangements.

2 (Example) The Managing Director has arranged a reception.
Really? I understood he hadn't arranged a reception.

3 The Swiss Minister of Trade will be here for the afternoon, of course.
Really? I understood he would be here for the whole day.

4 And the Board are going to be here.
Really? I understood they weren't going to be here.

5 Mr Heine has postponed the sales conference.
Really? I understood he hadn't postponed the sales conference.

6 The delegation want to see the new factory, of course.
Really? I understood they wanted to see the R & D section.

7 They'll have to be met at the airport, don't forget.
Really? I understood they wouldn't have to be met at the airport.

8 Well, we'll know definitely soon. Mr Gräber is going to draw up a programme.
Really? I understood Mr Heine was going to draw up a programme.

Drill 2

Mr Shermann is always wanting to make changes in office routine. But his secretary, Miss Jones, is rather conservative; she likes things just as they are.

1 (Example) I'm thinking of adopting a new filing system, Miss Jones.
Oh, I don't think it would be advisable to adopt a new filing system.

2 (Example) Would it help you if we bought a letter-opening machine?
Oh, I don't think there would be much sense in buying a letter-opening machine.

3 Or perhaps you'd like to have a telephone-answering machine.
Oh, I don't think it would be useful to have a telephone-answering machine.

4 I might be taking on another audio-typist. How would you feel about that?
Oh, I don't think there would be much point in taking on another audio-typist.

5 We're doing a lot of collating. What about hiring a collating machine?
Oh, I don't think there would be much advantage in hiring a collating machine.

6 It's about time we increased the petty cash float. What do you think?
Oh, I don't think it would be a good idea to increase the petty cash float.

7 I think we'd better get a new dictation machine don't you?
Oh, I don't think there would be much use in getting a new dictation machine.

8 Miss Jones, how would you like to work flexible hours?
Oh, I don't think it would be beneficial to work flexible hours.

Pronunciation Practice

In the last unit you practised questions beginning with question words, making your voice go down at the end. Like this:

When are you leaving?

That's the sort of question you might ask your boss because you need the information to enter in your diary. You really want to know the answer. What would happen if you made your voice go up instead of down, like this:

When are you leaving?

That's the sort of question you might ask a visitor when you're making polite conversation with him. You don't really need the answer. You're only asking out of interest or in order to keep the conversation going. We sometimes call this 'cocktail party' intonation. Listen to the two intonation patterns again.

When are you leaving?
I need information. Down.

When are you leaving?
Polite interest. Up. Now you try making the difference between these two patterns. Listen and repeat the questions in your book. First, asking for information. Down at the end.

When are you leaving?   *What did you see there?*
Where are you going?   *Who did you speak to?*
Which was the best one?   *When's he arriving?*

And now 'cocktail party' intonation. Up at the end.

When are you leaving?   *What did you see there?*
Where are you going?   *Who did you speak to?*
Which was the best one?   *When's he arriving?*

Practise that until you can really make a difference between the two patterns. When you have done that, go on to the limerick for this unit. Listen to it first.

Our cleaner, Miss White, had retired,
So a new one called May had been hired.
All files lying about
She picked up and threw out.
I'm afraid the next day May was fired.

Dialogue

Miss Schmidt is ringing the Imperial Hotel to make a complaint.

Receptionist: Imperial Hotel. Can I help you?

Miss Schmidt: Good morning. This is Schweibur GmbH. I'm ringing about an invoice you've sent us.

Receptionist: Oh, yes?

Miss Schmidt: It's for a single room and bath for a Mr Morovo on the 10th of this month.

Receptionist: Just a moment. Yes, that's right.

Miss Schmidt: I'm afraid Mr Morovo wasn't given a private bathroom in spite of the fact that we booked one for him in advance.

Receptionist: Oh, according to our records he *was* given a private bathroom.

Miss Schmidt: Well, I can assure you he wasn't given one. We did point the fact out to you at the time.

Receptionist: Well, I'll look into the matter straightaway then, and correct the invoice.

Miss Schmidt: It isn't the first time this has happened, you know.

Receptionist: OK, I'll sort it out. I'm sorry about this.

Miss Schmidt: That's alright. We'll expect to hear from you then. Goodbye.

Correspondence

In this Key suggestions for an acceptable version are printed in bold type.

Dear Mr Schumann,

Thank you for your letter of 2nd August. I hope that the Fonomat switchboard is now working correctly and you **will have** no further trouble with faulty components. **Please accept** our apologies for the **inconvenience** you have suffered.

I am pleased to be able to inform you that the LP **equipment has now been tested** and proved satisfactory. I am sure **there** will be no difficulty **in installing** the **equipment** by the end of the month. There are also one or two matters concerning the guarantee we **need/shall need** to talk over with you. May I *(omit)* suggest sometime during the third week of August if that is **convenient for** you?

I **enclose** a copy of the proposed guarantee and I would be grateful if you **could** find time to have a look at it before we **see** you. I also **intend** to send you the **information** on the Fonacopy that you requested. Is there any point **in our arranging** a demonstration at this stage?

Hoping to hear from you soon.

Yours sincerely,

Telegrams

A lot of employees are off sick with the flu. We are therefore badly behind schedule in the production of the Fonacopy.

We are investigating this matter with the Accounts Department and will cable the answer to your question as soon as possible.

1. NOT CUSTOMS RESPONSIBILITY DECIDE IF GOODS EXEMPT STOP CONTROL CERTIFICATE YOUR RESPONSIBILITY STOP

2. BARCLAYS REQUESTING RECEIPT STOP ORIGINAL DOCUMENTS ALL WITH YOU STOP PLEASE SETTLE WITH BANK STOP

Language Laboratory Part 2: Tapescript

Drill 3

Because Schweibur's telephonists are rather inefficient, Miss Jones sometimes has calls directed to her which she cannot deal with.

1 (Example) Oh, hallo. I'd like to place an order.
   I'm afraid this office doesn't deal with the placing of orders.

2 (Example) Good morning. Van Ek here. I'm calling about an invoice you've sent us.
   I'm afraid this office doesn't deal with the sending of invoices.

3 This is Farouk's of Cairo. It's about some goods you've shipped us.
   I'm afraid this office doesn't deal with the shipping of goods.

4 Morning. I'm ringing about a visit you arranged.
   I'm afraid this office doesn't deal with the arranging of visits.

Now, when Miss Jones has explained that the caller is talking to the wrong person, she then has to redirect the caller to the right department.

1 (Example) Oh, hallo. I'd like to place an order.
   I'm afraid this office doesn't deal with the placing of orders. But if you'll hold the line, I'll put you through to the Sales Department.

2 (Example) Good morning. Van Ek here. I'm calling about an invoice you've sent us.
   I'm afraid this office doesn't deal with the sending of invoices. But if you'll hold the line, I'll put you through to the Accounts Department.

3 This is Farouk's of Cairo. It's about some goods you've shipped to us.
   I'm afraid this office doesn't deal with the shipping of goods. But if you'll hold the line, I'll put you through to the Transport Department.

4 Morning. I'm ringing about a visit you arranged.
   I'm afraid this office doesn't deal with the arranging of visits. But if you'll hold the line, I'll put you through to the Visitors Department.

5 Hallo. About the placing of those advertisements you spoke of.
   I'm afraid this office doesn't deal with the placing of advertisements. But if you'll hold the line, I'll put you through to our Public Relations Officer.

6 Johannesson AB here. There's a slight problem with the supplies you're buying from us.
   I'm afraid this office doesn't deal with the buying of supplies. But if you'll hold the line, I'll put you through to the Purchasing Department.

7 Good morning. It's about our contract. We'd like to know if it's been drafted yet.
   I'm afraid this office doesn't deal with the drafting of contracts. But if you'll hold the line, I'll put you through to our Legal Adviser.

8 Hallo, Cardenali here. I asked for some information on stocks and you were checking them for me.
   I'm afraid this office doesn't deal with the checking of stocks. But if you'll hold the line, I'll put you through to the Head Storeman.

Drill 4

Schweibur's Sales Manager, Mr Heine, often gives his secretary, Miss Wood, information which she has to pass on to other people.

1. (Example) Hasn't that consignment been dispatched yet, Miss Wood?
   Yes, Mr Heine asked me to tell you it was dispatched yesterday.

2. (Example) You haven't heard when they're holding the management meeting, have you?
   Yes, Mr Heine asked me to tell you it's being held next Wednesday.

3. Did your boss circulate that report, by the way?
   Yes, Mr Heine asked me to tell you it was circulated last Friday.

4. Those plans I mentioned, have they been approved yet?
   Yes, Mr Heine asked me to tell you they were approved at yesterday's meeting.

5. Don't tell me they're going to postpone the sales conference.
   Yes, Mr Heine asked me to tell you it's being postponed until June 8th.

6. Oh, Miss Wood, do you know when they're going to discuss the budget?
   Yes, Mr Heine asked me to tell you it's being discussed at the next management meeting.

7. Did they appoint that new man incidentally?
   Yes, Mr Heine asked me to tell you he was appointed three days ago.

8. What I'd like to know is aren't we going to launch the sales campaign pretty soon?
   Yes, Mr Heine asked me to tell you it's being launched in July.

Active Listening

Passage 1: A customer is ringing the Sales Department.

Miss Wood: Mr Heine's office, good morning.

Blanco: Ah, good morning. My name is Blanco. I'm ringing from Barcelona. Can I speak to Mr Heine, please?

Miss Wood: I'm afraid Mr Heine isn't here at the moment. Can I take a message?

Blanco: Yes, tell him, please, I have just received the consignment of what I expected to be XJ30s and find they are in fact XJ40s. Now this was made quite clear, there's no excuse, and if I don't get those 30s by the end of the week there'll be trouble and we shall cancel the order under the terms of the contract. Have you got that?

Miss Wood: Yes, I'll give the message to Mr Heine, and I'm very sorry about this.

Blanco: OK. Goodbye.

Miss Wood: Goodbye.

What is the message Miss Wood should give Mr Heine?
Mr Blanco from Barcelona rang to complain that he has received a consignment of XJ40s instead of the required XJ30s. If he doesn't get the 30s by the end of the week he'll cancel the order under the terms of the contract.

Passage 2: Your boss is not in today but he recorded some instructions for you on the dictaphone.

Letter to Farouk's of Cairo. Send off a routine acknowledgement of their order, adding that we await the shipping instructions of their agents in Zurich. That to go off today.

What are you to do?
Send a routine letter of acknowledgement to Farouk's, stating that we await shipping instructions from their agents in Zurich.

Passage 3: Here is another instruction from your boss.

Letter to John Sheppard, Birmingham. Thank him for his application. Tell him that unfortunately we have no vacancies in his field at the moment, but that we shall keep his application on file. Should a suitable vacancy arise in the near future, we shall get in touch.

What are you to do?
Thank John Sheppard for his application but inform him that we regret there are no vacancies in his field at the moment. However, his application will be kept on file and he will be informed if a suitable vacancy arises in the near future.

Passage 4: Now listen to the last instruction from you boss.

I've decided to go to Belgrade on Tuesday next week, not Wednesday as originally planned. Can you get my tickets changed accordingly, but same time of departure, same hotel, etc, and also give Klein a ring and tell him of the change.

What are you to do?
Change the boss's travel arrangements to Tuesday instead of Wednesday. Keep all the details the same. Inform Klein by phone of the change.

Role Simulation

Situation

The students are asked to imagine that they have a visitor in their office. It is their task to make helpful suggestions or offer assistance to the visitor if he needs it.

Preparation

The teacher should play the part of the visitor throughout. The secretaries should respond to the visitor's statement by making helpful suggestions or offering assistance.

Teacher's Roles

1 D'you mind if I sit down for a few minutes? I'm not feeling at all well. (Unnecessary to call doctor now, but would like appointment for this evening.)

2 Heavens, is that the time? I'm never going to get back into the centre in time for my next appointment.

3 Look, I'm not sure what to do about this. I think it's a parking fine.

4 I always like to see a good film while I'm here. D'you know what's on at the moment?

5 Oh, I seem to have lost all those brochures your boss gave me. I wonder where I could have left them?

6 I've got about four hours to spare tomorrow afternoon. I'd like to see something of historic interest in the town.

7 I'm very sorry I won't be able to play any tennis while I'm here, but it just wasn't possible to bring my stuff with me.

8 Well, it doesn't matter so much about the briefcase—it was an old one anyway—but what is really serious is that all my traveller's cheques were in it. I'm not sure what to do next.

9 Well, I'm not too happy about the hotel. I haven't got a private bathroom and the room I'm in is rather noisy.

10 I've just discovered that I've come away without my address book. I'll have to get in touch with my office.

Key to 'What is this?'

Page 89: wastepaper bin
Page 93: first-aid box
Page 96: bandages and plasters

Unit Summary   135

Unit 9

Unit Summary

Introductory Recording	This episode is entitled 'Talking to a Visitor'. Mary Malone has been asked to welcome a visitor and talk to him until Mr Gräber is free.
Text	The Text is an article and a memo about the potential market in the Malapropezian Islands. This is the subject which is being discussed by Mr Gräber and his visitor.
Vocabulary	There is one exercise on vocabulary within the area of advertising.
Structures	1 Reported questions (Exercise B)
	2 Phrasal verbs with *go* (Exercise C and Drill 2)
	3 Prepositions followed by the gerund (Exercise D) Would you be interested *in* look*ing* round the factory?
Pronunciation Practice	There is an exercise on the intonation of repeated questions. This is followed by repetition of a limerick practising the vowel sound [aʊ] as in *down*.
Dialogue	The situation is that of giving directions on how to get to a place.
Correspondence	There is a draft letter to be corrected.
Telegrams	There are four telegrams, two to be decoded and two to be encoded.
Gambits	Drill 3: Passing on a request *Mr Heine wonders if you would mind . . . , Mr . . . ?* Drill 4: Encouraging or discouraging callers *Well, Mr Gräber's rather busy today. I doubt if he'll have time to . . .* *Well, Mr Gräber's quite busy today, but if you'd like to call back in half an hour he'll probably be able to . . .*
Active Listening	There are two passages in this unit.
	1 Comprehension of a recorded instruction
	2 Dictation of a letter
Role Simulation	The students are asked to imagine that they are faced with an awkward situation. They have to deal tactfully and diplomatically with the visitor

in the situation outlined in their role. The teacher plays the part of the visitor throughout.

Homework

No new written gambits are introduced. The student has to write a letter from the outline provided. She should draw on the gambits she has already met in the course.

Introductory Recording

Tapescript

Talking to a visitor

Mr Gräber is expecting a visitor this morning, but is on the phone at the moment. Mary Malone has been asked to welcome the visitor and talk to him until Mr Gräber is free, and to deal with any other callers.

Malone: Good morning. Mr Gräber's office. Can I help you?

Fromm: Ah, good morning. I'd like to speak to Mr Gräber, please.

Malone: Can I have your name, please?

Fromm: Fromm. In the Buying Section. Upstairs.

Malone: Ah, yes. I'm afraid Mr Gräber has rather a lot to get through this morning, Mr Fromm. He has a meeting with a visitor from Djakarta, and some urgent enquiries to go into. I doubt actually if Mr Gräber will be available before 2.30. Would you like to call back, perhaps?

Fromm: Yes, I'll certainly do that. You will tell Mr Gräber that I called, won't you?

Malone: Yes, I will. I've got your name down. Thank you. Goodbye.

Fromm: Yes, goodbye.

Delft: Good morning.

Malone: Oh, good morning. Mr Delft? From Djakarta?

Delft: Yes, that's right. I think Mr Gräber's expecting me.

Malone: Yes, he's in the office, but I'm afraid he's on the phone at the moment. He wondered if you'd mind taking a seat for a moment.

Delft: Yes, OK, of course I can wait. It's taken me two days to get here. A few more minutes won't make any difference.

Malone: Are you actually from Djakarta?

Delft: Well, that's where the office is, of course. But right now I'm on sales research. Doing a project. I've been on tour to various parts of South East Asia and the West Pacific recently. In fact, I've just travelled here from Malapropezia. But I don't expect you've heard of that. Not many people have.

Introductory Recording

Malone: Erm, no, I'm afraid I don't know where that is. I did study geography at school, but I can never remember which countries are where in that part of the world.

Delft: I wouldn't worry too much about it if I were you. You'll get by without knowing, I should think.

Malone: Yes. Was your, er, research successful?

Delft: Depends what you mean by successful. But it was interesting alright. Er, I was asked, you see, to study what the markets are like in those out-of-the-way parts of the world. For our products, that is. So I've been going round, assessing the market—seeing what it's like. You know. And certainly the markets are there. But the question is what they're like as long-term prospects. Will they last? That's what I've got to get across to Mr Gräber today. They certainly look good right now, the markets, but I'm just not sure how good they're going to be in the long-term. Still, I must be boring you with all this stuff. It's not your problem is it?

Malone: Oh, and why not? No, I'm really very interested in keeping up to date. And I'm sure Mr Gräber will want to go through your research results very carefully with you.

Delft: Well, you know, I'm not sure exactly what his interest is in all this. I wasn't told exactly what he wants to know. But I expect I'll soon find out, won't I? How do you get on with Mr Gräber yourself?

Malone: Well, I'm not sure whether I should say. But, yes, he's a very pleasant person to work for.

Delft: Yes, I see. Oh, and I meant to ask you, what time do you, er, get off tonight?

Malone: It's usually about 5.30. Why?

Delft: Well, er, this is the first time I've been in Zurich, you see, and I haven't really much idea what the places are to see and where to go and so on. In fact, I'm not even sure where my hotel is. So I wondered . . . I wondered if you, er, might like to come out and have a drink and then perhaps we could go on and have a meal. You know. I'd like that . . .

Malone: Er, well, so would I, and that's very kind of you. But I've already made plans for this evening. I'm sorry.

Delft: Oh, that's OK. Some other time perhaps. Er, by the way, talking of the hotel, I'm not exactly sure where it is. It's the . . . Oh, just a second, I've got it written down somewhere. Yes, here. It's the Nova Park. Know where that is?

Malone: Oh, yes. It's the big one in the centre of the city. Erm, actually, perhaps the best idea would be for me to order a taxi for you. Or you could walk. I'll see what time there is when you've finished talking with . . .

Malone: Excuse me a moment. Hello?

Gräber: Er, Mary, if Mr Delft is here, send him in, yes? And will you come in yourself? We'll need some notes and there'll be a memo to send round later.

Malone: Er, would you like to come this way, Mr Delft. I'll tell you about reaching the hotel after your meeting, all right?

Gräber: Ah, Mr Delft, welcome. Mary been looking after you alright, yes?

Delft: Oh yes, very well, Mr Gräber.

Gräber: Yes, of course. She's good at that. I don't know what I would do without her. Now then . . .

Comprehension Questions

1. When Mr Fromm rang, why didn't Mary Malone put him through to Mr Gräber?
   Because Mr Gräber had a lot to get through that morning. (He had a meeting with a visitor and then some urgent enquiries to go into.)

2. Why can't Mr Delft go straight into the meeting with Mr Gräber?
   Because Mr Gräber's on the phone.

3. Where does Mr Delft normally work?
   In Djakarta.

4. What has he been doing recently?
   He's been on tour to various parts of South East Asia (and the West Pacific).

5. Mr Delft has just come back from Malapropezia. What was he doing there?
   Studying / Assessing the market for Schweibur's products there.

6. What does he think about the opportunities?
   He thinks they're good but he's not sure how good they're going to be in the long term.

7. What does Mr Delft try to find out from Mary?
   What sort of person Mr Gräber is.

8. What does Mr Delft want Mary to do?
   He wants her to come out for a drink and a meal with him that night.

9. What is Mary's reaction to his invitation?
   She refuses politely.

10. What does Mary suggest she should do to help Mr Delft?
    She suggests she should order a taxi to take him to his hotel after the meeting.

Text: An Article and a Memo

Comprehension Questions

The words and phrases in italics are quoted verbatim from the Text.

1. Was modern civilization essential to the Malapropezians?
   No, *they managed to get by without it*.

2. When was contact with the islanders first made?
   In the 18th century.

3. How was contact with the islands maintained?
   Passing ships would occasionally drop anchor in one of the bays.

4. Why was trade with the islands never developed?
   Because *it was found that the only exportable commodity on the islands was conch shells*.

5. How did the islanders react when the sailors offered them glass beads?
   They *showed a marked lack of enthusiasm* for them.

6. What happened from then on?
   The islanders were left to go their own way without interference from the outside world.

7. Why did the American travel agents want to develop the Malapropezians?
   So that they would have *an alternative to Hawaii to offer their more discriminating clients*.

8. Were the islanders shy with strangers for very long?
   No, *it did not take long for them to overcome their shyness*.

9. Why did they agree on the development of the tourist trade?
   The realized *that transistor radios and Honda motorcycles were a vast improvement on glass beads*.

10. When did the islanders become totally converted to the notion of progress?
    When the casino was opened.

11. How was the oil discovered?
    Two Australian businessmen went off to explore the interior.

12. What advantage have these resources over the North Sea oil fields?
    They are *easy to get at*.

13. What has attracted all the foreign embassies and the big companies to to islands?
    The enormous potential for trade and industry.

14. What does the Managing Director of Schweibur want to know?
    What they are *going to do about opening up a markt* for their *products in the Malapropezians*.

15. What did he ask Erich Gräber?
    Whether they *intended to carry out a market survey in the near future*.

16 What facts does Mr Gräber want to find out about the newspapers?
    How many there are and how big their circulation is.

17 How else might they advertise their products?
    Through trade journals and by sending out *sales literature direct to prospective buyers* (by sending out *direct mail shots*).

18 What might it be better to do?
    It might be better to *put the whole matter into the hands of an advertising agency.*

19 What two things is Mr Gräber not sure about?
    He's not sure *if the Malapropezian government has imposed any trade restrictions or whether they limit the export of foreign exchange.*

Key to the Exercises

Exercise A

When a company wants to *open up* a new market in a foreign country, it often carries out a market *survey/study*. Obviously, the company must make sure that a *potential* market for its products exists and that the *prospective/potential* buyers have sufficient *purchasing power* to buy the goods. The seller must also be aware of any trade *restrictions* which might affect his sales. For example, some governments limit the amount of goods that can be imported into the country by imposing *quotas* and others may limit the amount of *foreign exchange* that can be transferred to the company's home account. Once these questions have been settled satisfactorily, the company must decide what the best way to *promote/publicize* its products is. They may *insert* advertisements in newspapers or in *trade journals* that specialize in their type of goods. But these should have a high *circulation* to ensure good coverage. On the other hand, they may prefer to send sales *literature* direct to would-be customers. This is known as a direct *mail shot*. If the company goes all out to sell its products, it will *launch* an intensive advertising *campaign*. The company may well commission an advertising *agency* to handle the whole matter for them.

Exercise B

1 Mr Braun wanted to know if you talked/had talked to Lemelle's representative.
2 Mr Boileau asked who dealt/deals with discrepancies in our accounts.
3 Mr Schulz wondered whether we should ask an advertising agency to handle the campaign.
4 Mr Flügel enquired why you hadn't circulated the agenda for the next meeting.
5 Mr Heine wanted to find out if he could/can allow Mertons a 10% discount.
6 Mr Shermann asked when we were reviewing our latest project.

Key to the Exercises

7 Mr Hoffmann wanted to know who you spoke/had spoken to at the Ministry of Trade.
8 Mr Grauberg enquired why the latest sales figures were/are so discouraging.
9 Mr Boileau wanted to be told if Jackson's had broken their contract.
10 Miss Lachenal asked if she had to consult the branches before going ahead.

Exercise C

Possible answers.

1 To ensure that everyone understands, *go over* the instructions twice.
2 We haven't time *to go into* all the details.
3 Sales *went up* last month.
4 The value of the dollar *has gone down* recently.
5 After the meeting he *went off* to catch his plane.
6 He told me *to go on with* the typing.
7 He was so busy today that he *went without* his lunch.
8 They said we *had gone back on* our agreement.
9 As soon as permission is granted, we *will go ahead with* the new building.
10 I wonder if they *will go through with* the deal?

Exercise D

1 We very much look forward *to hearing* from you.
2 We are well aware of the advantages *of ordering* in bulk.
3 I'm afraid we can't rely *on receiving* the goods on time.
4 We are used *to dealing* with such difficulties.
5 Unfortunately we have not yet succeeded *in tracing* the fault.
6 They have accused us *of putting up* our prices unreasonably.
7 We have every intention *of sending* you samples of our latest product.
8 There's a good case *for setting up* a joint working party.
9 We must insist *on receiving* immediate payment.

Language Laboratory Part 1: Tapescript

Drill 1

Mr Heine's secretary has to deal with a lot of telephone enquiries. Sometimes she is unable to answer the questions that are put to her.

1 (Example) Robertson speaking. Where is Mr Heine?
I'm sorry Mr Robertson, but I don't know where he is.

2 (Example) Sykes here. Will the goods be despatched tomorrow?
I'm sorry Mr Sykes, but I doubt whether they will be dispatched tomorrow.

3 My name's Fraser. Did Mr Heine get my letter?
I'm sorry Mr Fraser, but I'm not sure whether he got your letter.

4 Betty, this is Marianne. Which file did Mr Heine take away?
I'm sorry Marianne, but I can't remember which file he took away.

5 This is Davis speaking. How much discount can I get on my order?
I'm sorry Mr Davis, but I'm not certain how much discount you can get on it.

6 My name's Grant. Did Mr Heine meet my representative?
I'm sorry Mr Grant, but I couldn't tell you whether he met your representative.

7 Flügel speaking. Which invoice does Mr Heine want?
I'm sorry Mr Flügel, but I don't know which invoice he wants.

8 Brown here. When will the next conference be held?
I'm sorry Mr Brown, but I haven't been told when it will be held.

Drill 2

Mr Flügel is discussing one or two problems with his secretary.

1 (Example) There seem to be several discrepancies in this account. Perhaps we should take another look at the invoices.
Yes, I'm afraid we'll have to go through them.

2 (Example) The cost of living has risen steeply in the last six months. I think we're going to need another increase in wages.
Yes, I'm afraid they'll have to go up.

3 I wish I could have a rest from all this work, but I suppose I'll just have to continue it.
Yes, I'm afraid you'll have to go on with it.

4 I've had a lot of complaints about this recently. I suppose I should investigate the matter.
Yes, I'm afraid you'll have to go into it.

5 Everyone is having doubts about this contract. But we'll have to keep to it now.
Yes, I'm afraid we'll have to go through with it.

6 They're very angry that we're breaking the agreement. But what else can we do in the circumstances?
Yes, I'm afraid we'll have to go back on it.

7 I still have some doubt about the plan, but I suppose I can't delay it any longer.
Yes, I'm afraid you'll have to go ahead with it.

8 The meeting starts just after midday. It looks as though you won't have time for lunch.
No, I'm afraid I'll have to go without it.

Pronunciation Practice

In the last two units we've been practising questions that begin with question words like *who*, *where* and *what*. Remember, when you ask a question because you need information, your voice goes down at the end.

Language Laboratory Part 1

Like this:

When are you leaving?

And when you ask simply in order to make polite conversation, your voice goes up at the end. Like this:

When are you leaving?

Now, what happens when you have to repeat your question? Suppose you don't catch what the person says and you have to ask him again, what kind of intonation do you use? Listen to this:

When are you leaving?
(incoherent answer)
When are you leaving, did you say?

Did you notice how the speaker's voice kept going up and up when she repeated her question? It's different from the polite 'cocktail party' intonation because your voice starts rising right from the beginning of the question and not just at the end. Now practise these two intonation patterns. Listen and repeat the questions in your book.

When is he due to arrive?
When is he due to arrive, did you say?

What is the name of the street?
What is the name of the street, did you say?

Where will the meeting be held?
Where will the meeting be held, did you say?

Which of the files do you need?
Which of the files do you need, did you say?

What is the time of his flight?
What is the time of his flight, did you say?

Practise that until you can do it really naturally. When you have done that, go on to the limerick for this unit. Listen to it first.

She paid us and left with a flounce,
Then the bank rang us up to announce:
'She's not got that amount
In her current account,
So that cheque for a thousand'll bounce.'

Dialogue

Mr Heine comes across to Sweden fairly regularly to see Miss Lindfors' boss. He is just leaving the office now and is asking Miss Lindfors to direct him to the nearest bus stop.

Mr Heine: Well, thank you very much for all your help, Miss Lindfors. I'm afraid I didn't bring my car with me this time, so could you tell me how to get to the nearest bus stop?

Miss Lindfors: Certainly. Turn left when you leave this building and take the path leading to the next block of offices.

Mr Heine: That's not the main way out, is it?

Miss Lindfors: No, this will take you to a side gate. Turn right as you go out and walk along the road until you come to a petrol station.

Mr Heine: Ah, yes, I remember seeing that on the way here.

Miss Lindfors: Just beyond that there's a busy crossroads.

Mr Heine: Ah, that must be the intersection with the main road.

Miss Lindfors: Yes, it is. Turn right again and the bus stop is just round the corner. You can't miss it. It's opposite a restaurant.

Mr Heine: Now, let's see if I've got this straight. Left at the front door. Right at the side gate, then walk as far as the crossroads. Then right again.

Miss Lindfors: Yes, that's right, Mr Heine. I don't think you'll have any difficulty finding it. It's about five minutes' walk from here.

Mr Heine: Good. Well, I must be off. Thank you again for all your assistance.

Miss Lindfors: Don't mention it. I hope you have a good trip back.

Correspondence

In this Key suggestions for an acceptable version are printed in bold type.

Dear Sirs,

Further to your telephone call yesterday, we have decided to go **ahead** with our **advertising** campaign in Malapropezia and would be interested **in placing** an advertisement in the 'Malapropezian Trade Journal'.

I understand that the journal **is** published monthly, but I would be grateful if you could tell me how big **your circulation is** and where **your main sales are**. We have come to the conclusion that a series of six **insertions** should give us sufficient **coverage** and be **considerably** cheaper than a quarterly advertisement. However, before we confirm this we should like you to quote your rates for a quarterly **insertion** and for a monthly **insertion**.

I believe I am right **in saying** that you would translate the text for us. If this **is** the case, how soon **would you** require our copy? Could you also let us know **in which issue we could place our first advertisement**?

We look forward to **hearing** from you.

Yours faithfully,

Telegrams

We don't understand the order you have placed with us. We don't produce that item. Please clarify your order.

We made a mistake when we placed our order (reference number 416). We wanted to order 500 LM7s.

1. REQUIRE MINIMUM ORDER FIVE HUNDRED TO MANUFACTURE YOUR SPECIAL PAPERWEIGHTS STOP

2. PLEASE SPEED UP TRANSPORTATION AND CUSTOMS IN LIBYA STOP NUMEROUS CUSTOMER COMPLAINTS STOP

Language Laboratory Part 2: Tapescript

Drill 3

People often ring up or call at the Sales Department to speak to Mr Heine, Schweibur's Sales Manager. Mr Heine often wants people to wait for a moment or ring back, and his secretary, Miss Wood, has to pass these requests on to the caller.

1. (Example) Shermann? Ask him to call back later, would you?
   Mr Heine wonders if you would mind calling back later, Mr Shermann?

2. (Example) Nelson, is it? Tell him to take a seat for a moment.
   Mr Heine wonders if you would mind taking a seat for a moment, Mr Nelson?

3. Not Thompson again! Can you ask him to make an appointment for later in the week?
   Mr Heine wonders if you would mind making an appointment for later in the week, Mr Thompson?

4. Hoffmann? He'll have to wait a few moments, I'm afraid.
   Mr Heine wonders if you would mind waiting a few moments, Mr Hoffmann?

5. Oh dear. I can't speak to Gonzales now. Ask him to ring back in about an hour, could you?
   Mr Heine wonders if you would mind ringing back in about an hour, Mr Gonzales?

6. Ah, yes. Could you please ask Mr Boileau to look in on me some time this afternoon.
   Mr Heine wonders if you would mind looking in on him some time this afternoon, Mr Boileau?

7. Well, just ask Mr Andersson to hold the line a second.
   Mr Heine wonders if you would mind holding the line a second, Mr Andersson?

8   Konstanz, is it? I'm afraid I'll have to ask him to postpone the discussion until tomorrow.
    Mr Heine wonders if you would mind postponing the discussion until tomorrow, Mr Konstanz?

Drill 4   Mr Gräber is kept very busy at the office and it's his secretary's job to see that he is not constantly interrupted by people he doesn't want to see.

1   (Example)   I was wondering if I could just have a word with Mr Gräber about an order.
    Well, Mr Gräber's rather busy today. I doubt if he'll have time to have a word with you.

2   (Example)   Can you tell me if Mr Gräber will be able to give me an answer today?
    Well, Mr Gräber's rather busy today. I doubt if he'll have time to give you an answer.

3   Look, I know I haven't got an appointment but I thought I'd just see if I could speak to Mr Gräber.
    Well, Mr Gräber's rather busy today. I doubt if he'll have time to speak to you.

4   Just thought I'd ring to find out whether Gräber's ready to discuss the market survey.
    Well, Mr Gräber's rather busy today. I doubt if he'll have time to discuss the market survey.

Sometimes the secretary thinks that Mr Gräber would be interested in seeing the caller. In these cases she encourages the person to call back again later.

1   (Example)   Sorry I didn't arrange this before, but d'you think Mr Gräber could give me an appointment today?
    Well, Mr Gräber is quite busy today, but if you'd like to call back in half an hour he'll probably be able to give you an appointment.

2   (Example)   Just wondered if I could pop in and see Mr Gräber today.
    Well, Mr Gräber is quite busy today, but if you'd like to call back in half an hour he'll probably be able to see you.

3   Can I bring these samples round? I'd like Mr Gräber to have a look at them.
    Well, Mr Gräber is quite busy today, but if you'd like to call back in half an hour he'll probably be able to have a look at them.

4   D'you think Mr Gräber could spare a moment to help me with the plans?
    Well, Mr Gräber's quite busy today, but if you'd like to call back in half an hour he'll probably be able to help you with the plans.

Now, using the notes to guide you, either encourage or discourage these callers.

Language Laboratory Part 2

1. I was wondering if I could just have a word with Mr Gräber about an order.
Well, Mr Gräber's rather busy today. I doubt if he'll have time to have a word with you.

2. Can you tell me if Mr Gräber will be able to give me an answer today?
Well, Mr Gräber's quite busy today, but if you'd like to call back in half an hour he'll probably be able to give you an answer.

3. Look, I know I haven't got an appointment, but I thought I'd just see if I could speak to Mr Gräber.
Well, Mr Gräber's quite busy today, but if you'd like to call back in half an hour he'll probably be able to speak to you.

Active Listening

Passage 1: Mr Gräber has gone to France for a few days. Before leaving, he recorded this message for his secretary.

The only really important thing coming up is that phone call from Wagner in Hanover. He'll probably ring this week, and when he does, put him through to Heine. Warn Heine that you're going to do this, and give him the necessary file.

What is his secretary to do?
Warn Mr Heine that he will probably have to deal with a call from Mr Wagner in Hanover while Mr Gräber is away. Give him the necessary file (in advance).

Passage 2: Your boss has dictated a letter on to a dictation machine for you to type out.

Dear Jake. That's spelt J-A-K-E, ah, and address this letter care of the Chase Manhatten Bank in New York will you? At a recent meeting of our Board of Directors it was decided to go—no, cancel that—it was decided that our company should—er—go carefully into the business—delete that business—the matter of opening up a new market for our products in the South Pacific. Erm—As you know, recent events in that part of the world have happened—no, taken place so rapidly that we haven't really had time to erm study these islands and know very little about the people there. However, we feel that—er, no start again. However, it would be extremely foolish of us not to take advantage of the tremendous upsurge in trade produced by the recent discovery of oil on some of the islands. That area of the world is developing so fast that to hold back at this stage would be disastrous for an expanding company like ours. Nevertheless, we are somewhat hesitant about launching a—no, delete those last two words—about entering a totally unknown market. We therefore feel that before we go ahead with an advertising campaign, it would be wiser to get sound advice from someone who has already had some dealings with these people and can pinpoint some of the problems that are likely to arise. New para. When this matter was raised, I immediately thought of you with your long experience of trading in the Pacific, and the Board asked me to approach you about acting as a consultant to us, for which, of course, there—no, cancel that—you would be paid generous fees. I do appreciate that you have many other commitments. Nevertheless, I hope you will, er, feel able to consider this offer. I know you are the one person who could get us thinking along the right lines. New para. Please let me have your reactions as soon as possible. Finish up with regards to both him and his wife. Yours sincerely and can you get this back to me as quickly as possible?

Write out the letter your boss has dictated.

Role Simulation

Situation The students are asked to imagine that they are faced with an awkward situation. It is their task to deal tactfully and diplomatically with the visitor in the situation outlined in their roles.

Preparation The teacher should study the roles given below and draw up his own role cards for the part of the visitor.

Procedure The teacher should play the part of the visitor throughout.

The secretaries should
1. apologize for the delay if there is one
2. act according to their roles.

Secretary's Roles

1. A Mr Devlin has called to see your boss. There is a slight delay. Explain and apologize. You know that Mr Devlin's brother and partner in the firm has just died. You should offer your condolences.

2. A Mr Kosic, a Russian, has called to see your boss. There is a slight delay. Explain and apologize. While he's waiting he tries to find out what research is done by your company, what government contracts they have and what new products your company is hoping to bring on the market. You must avoid giving him direct answers without being rude.

3. Your boss is ill and cannot keep an appointment with a Mr Neeskens from Holland. Explain and apologize. You should inform the visitor that your boss's assistant (invent a name) will see him instead. This does not please Mr Neeskens who would rather speak to the Marketing Manager. It is your job to convince him that the assistant is the best person to see.

4. A Mr Leclerc calls at the office expecting to see your boss. According to your diary his appointment is for the following day. He is convinced the mistake is yours and is very angry about it. You must apologize and make alternative arrangements.

5   An American called Mr Harriwell has called to see your boss. There is a slight delay. Explain and apologize. While he is waiting he tries to date you. He is very persistent. You are not married but he doesn't appeal to you.

6   Your boss is out of the office today. A Mr Jensen from the Danish subsidiary who is working temporarily at Headquarters has come into your office asking for a certain file. You know this file is confidential. Although he says he's sure your boss won't mind, you must refuse his request.

7   Mr Carr is a young Englishman who has applied for a job with your company. He is waiting in your office to go into an interview with your boss and is extremely nervous. He asks you all sorts of questions about your boss and tells you how important it is for him to get this job. You must try to put him at his ease.

8   A Mr Santos has called into the office. He wants to see your boss and says it's urgent, but he hasn't got an appointment. Furthermore, you know your boss cannot stand him and does not want to see him either now or at any other time. It is your job to get rid of Mr Santos as politely as possible.

9   Mr Kurz has called to see your boss. There is a slight delay. Explain and apologize. It is obvious that Mr Kurz has had too much to drink at his business lunch. He is one of these quarrelsome drunks. He insists that you should offer him a drink while he's waiting. He then proceeds to take a hip flask out of his pocket. Try and distract his attention.

10 The same Mr Kurz who was drinking merrily in the last role situation is now feeling extremely sick. He has just dashed out of a meeting with your boss and has asked to be directed to the nearest 'Gentlemen's'. When he comes back you should offer him some help.

Key to 'What is this?'

Page 100: scissors
Page 101: razor blade
Page 102: penknife

Unit 10

Unit Summary

Introductory Recording

This episode is entitled 'The Transfer'. Mary Malone has suddenly been transferred to the Accounts Department, where she is working for Mr Flügel. Mr Flügel is instructing Mary to investigate a letter from a company in Birmingham, who are maintaining that Schweibur have overcharged them. Mary does not really understand what she has to do, but Mr Flügel is completely unsympathetic. The episode closes with Mary ringing up Alpair, who have recently advertised for a personal secretary.

Text

The Text is the letter that Mr Flügel asked Mary to investigate.

Vocabulary

There is one exercise on common phrases within the area of finance.

Structures

1. Connectors:
   However, nevertheless, in view of, consequently/therefore, furthermore/in addition (Exercise B)

2. Modals with past time reference: (Exercise C and Drill 1)
   He must have called while I was out.
   He could have left earlier.
   He may have told him.
   He might have mentioned it.
   He should have told us.
   He would have sent a message.

3. *Get* as a phrasal verb (Exercise D and Drill 2)

Pronunciation Practice

There is an exercise on the intonation pattern in alternative questions such as *Would you like tea or coffee?* and *Is the meeting on Monday or Tuesday?*

This is followed by repetition of a limerick and practising the vowel sound [ɔɪə] as in *employer*.

Dialogue

The situation is that of asking a customer for further information about his recent order.

Correspondence

There is a draft letter to be corrected.

Telegrams

There are four telegrams, two to be decoded and two to be encoded.

Gambits

Drill 3: Finding out information
Good morning. Mr Braun was wondering . . .

Unit Summary

Drill 4: Polite refusals
I'm afraid that's out of the question. We couldn't possibly . . .

Active Listening

There are four passages in this unit. Passages 1 and 2 are telephone messages to be taken, and Passages 3 and 4 are recorded instructions.

Role Simulation

The students are asked to imagine that their boss's opposite number from a subsidiary has come to their company for a period. He is sharing an office with their boss, who has asked them to explain to the newcomer where everything is kept and what the office procedure is.

Notes are provided for the students on the points they should cover during briefing of the newcomer.

The teacher should play the part of the newcomer.

Homework

This consists of accepting and refusing formal invitations. Model answers are provided for the student.

Introductory Recording

Tapescript

The Transfer
Mary Malone has suddenly been transferred to the Accounts Section. Her place in Mr Gräber's office has been taken by a temporary secretary. So when her friend Maureen rings, she gets a surprise.

Temp: Good afternoon, Mr Gräber's office.

Lynch: Hello. Is that you, Mary?

Temp: No, I'm afraid Miss Malone has been transferred. Can I help you?

Lynch: Oh no, it was just a personal matter. But can you tell me which section she's in now?

Temp: Yes, she's on extension 294. Working for Mr Flügel.

Lynch: Mr Flügel? In accounts? Oh, saints preserve us, she must have done something awful. Right. Thank you. I'll give her a ring there.

Malone: Mr Flügel's office. Can I help you?

Lynch: Mary, is that you? It's Maureen. What's happened? What have you been doing to get transferred there . . . ?

Malone: Oh, Maureen. Look, ring back later, will you? No better still, let's have lunch. One o'clock, alright?

Lynch: Yes, fine, of course. See you downstairs at one. 'Bye.

Malone: Yes. 'Bye.

Malone: Excuse me, Mr Flügel. What were you saying? About what may have happened?

Flügel: I said that there must have been a mistake. This letter from Birmingham. These people are suggesting we've overcharged them. And consequently they haven't paid their account in full. It's nonsense, of course. I want you to look into this matter, now, and straighten it out at once.

Malone: Well, er, financial matters have never been, er, I'm not very good at them . . .

Flügel: Oh, come, come. This must have been part of your training, surely. It's an important part of a good secretary's duties; now, listen carefully and I'll explain again. The first item that must be checked—this invoice number 13886. They say that they can't trace the order in their order book, and therefore the goods can't have been delivered to them. So your first step is to see who placed the order. Someone in Birmingham. Or it might have been an agent, I suppose. And see if you can find the dispatch record, to check on the forwarding agent, and so forth.

Malone: Ah, I was wondering, how should I start looking for the information . . .

Flügel: With your eyes, perhaps. Look, the records should be available for you. However, you may ask the clerks if you have to. But they're very busy, of course.

Malone: I was wondering if I might ask Mr Hoffmann to help me . . .

Flügel: Hoffmann? My deputy, you mean? No, that's out of the question. He must finish the management accounts by the end of the week. We couldn't possibly disturb him. No. You must use your own initiative and just get on with it.

Malone: Yes, Mr Flügel. I'll try.

Flügel: Good. Now. In addition, they say we should allow them a discount of 5 per cent, and we calculated it at only 2 ½ per cent. Nonsense again of course. However, better check the original correspondence and see what's happened.

Malone: Yes, Mr Flügel. I suppose we could have made a mistake . . .

Flügel: Most unlikely. This is a very efficient section, Miss Malone, that you have joined. Now. One final point. They're complaining about price increases on these 500 RMY units. I'm quite sure this must be related to changing rates in the pound sterling. There must have been a circular about it, too. Trace it, make a copy, and we'll put it in with our reply. Right?

Malone: Yes, Mr Flügel. And I wanted to ask you when you wanted this information. Er, . . .

Introductory Recording

Flügel: Oh, it's not really all that urgent, is it? First thing tomorrow morning will do.

Malone: Oh. Yes. I see. Right, Mr Flügel . . . *(Fade)*

Switchboard: Alpair.

Malone: Oh, good afternoon. I wanted to speak to someone about the job you advertised. For a personal secretary. In yesterday's paper . . . *(Fade)*

Comprehension Questions

1. Where has Mary been transferred?
   To the Accounts Department.

2. What was her friend's reaction to this when she heard of the transfer?
   She was horrified / She thought Mary must have done something awful.

3. What is Mary's new boss trying to get Mary to do?
   Look into a letter of complaint and straighten it out.

4. Is Mary confident that she can do this?
   No, she isn't.

5. What is Mr Flügel's attitude to her difficulties?
   He thinks she is being difficult, and that the task is an easy one.

6. What help does he give her?
   Very little.

7. Does he allow her to turn to anyone else for help?
   No, he doesn't, although the clerks may be able to help.

8. What is Mary's reaction to the conversation?
   She rings up Alpair about their advertisement for a personal secretary.

9. What would your reaction be in that situation?

Text: The Transfer

Comprehension Questions

The words and phrases in italics are quoted verbatim from the Text.

1. What have Jellicoe and Glossop received?
   Schweibur's *quarterly statement of account for all transactions up to 31st August*.

2. Why do they think there must have been some error?
   Because *the balance of £2,030 does not correspond with their books*.

3. How did they discover the discrepancies?
   By *going over the entries posted in the account*.

4. Why have they queried the debit of £267 against Invoice No 13886?
   Because they *have no record of such a bill* in their *files*.

5 What conclusion have they come to?
That these goods could not have been sent to them.

6 What accusation do they make in their second query?
They accuse Schweibur of *going back* on their *agreement of 5th November 1976*.

7 Why are they complaining about the 2½ per cent discount?
They think Schweibur *should have allowed* them *a discount of 5 per cent*.

8 When are discounts allowed?
When *payment is effected by the last day of the quarter*.

9 Why are they perturbed that RMY staplers cost £1.50 each?
Because *the last time* they *ordered this item the price per unit was quoted at £1.25*.

10 Why are Jellicoe and Glossop angry at this price rise?
They *feel strongly they should have been informed of the price rise*.

11 What might they have done if they'd known about it?
They *might have opted to cancel the order*.

12 Are they going to pay the account in full?
No, they *are deducting a total of £592*.

13 What are Jellicoe and Glossop instructing their bank to do?
They are instructing them to remit the sum of £1,411 in full settlement.

14 What do they want Schweibur to do when this money has been remitted?
They want them to issue a *receipt*.

Key to the Exercises

Exercise A
1 to raise an invoice
2 to remit a sum / payment / the balance
3 to allow a discount
4 to place an order
5 to dispatch goods
6 to post an entry / an account
7 to debit an account / the balance
8 to issue a receipt
9 to quote a price

Exercise B
1 None of the applicants for the job was at all suitable. *Therefore / consequently* we shall have to re-advertise the post.

2 Mr Flügel has to attend a meeting on Friday afternoon. *However*, he should be free to see you after four.

Key to the Exercises 155

3 The staff have complained bitterly about the catering service. *Furthermore,/ In addition,* there have been several instances of sickness as a result of eating in the canteen.

4 Their last two accounts have not been settled yet. *In view of this* I think we should withdraw their credit facilities.

5 We realize we are not allowed any say in Company policy. *Nevertheless* we feel we should be consulted when major decisions are taken.

6 Last year's figures on sales of this product were very high. *However*, there seems to have been a fall in demand this year.

8 Mr Gräber will not be able to attend our next meeting. *In view of this* I suggest we postpone discussing his report till next month.

9 One of the girls has been off for almost a fortnight. *Consequently,/ Therefore,* we are a bit behind with the typing.

10 The plans for the ceremony have been widely criticized. *Nevertheless*, it has been decided to go ahead with the existing arrangements.

Exercise C

1 We seem to have run out of carbon, I'm afraid.

Miss Miller: Oh, for heavens sake! You *might have told* me that yesterday. *I would/could have added* it to our monthly stationery order. You *should/ought to have noticed* that stocks were getting low, since it's your responsibility.

Miss Hyslop: But that's just it, Miss Miller, I'm quite sure we weren't low on carbon. We had another full box left. I think someone must have taken it.

Miss Miller: Oh, I see. I wonder who would want carbon paper. I suppose Mary *might/may/could have run short* yesterday, but surely she *wouldn't have borrowed* a whole box. Anyway, I'm sure she *would have left* a note to tell me. No, it *couldn't have been* her.

Miss Hyslop: Miss Jones *may/might/could have taken* some to type those reports.

Miss Miller: A whole box?

Miss Hyslop: No, it doesn't seem likely, does it? Oh, hang on a minute. Oh, it's still here after all, Miss Miller. It *must have fallen* behind that huge pile of copy paper. Oh, dear! I suppose I *should/ought to have looked* there in the first place.

Exercise D

Possible answers

1 I hope he *gets back* the case he lost.
2 He said I could *get off* an hour earlier on Friday.
3 They seem to be *getting on* very quickly *with* that pile of letters.

4 He hasn't *got over* the shock yet.
5 There are a number of ways of *getting round* the problem.
6 We *got through* two boxes of carbon last week.
7 I can't *get across* to him the urgency of the matter.
8 It's easier to *get at* than most places.
9 Don't worry, we'll *get by* somehow or other.
10 It was a bad line but I *got down* most of the message.

Language Laboratory Part 1: Tapescript

Drill 1

Two secretaries are talking together in the office.

1 (Example)   There's a visitor in the outer office.
  Oh, it must be Mr Matthews.

2 (Example)   I can't get through to Maureen. There's no reply.
  Oh, she must have gone off early.

3 Does this briefcase belong to Mr Gräber's visitor?
  Oh, he must have forgotten it.

4 Mary said she'd introduce him to us.
  Oh, she must know him.

5 There's no one left in the conference room.
  Oh, they must have finished.

6 Have you seen that file that was on my desk?
  Oh, I must have put it away.

7 He can't talk about anything except his job.
  Oh, he must like it.

8 Mr Heine put a whole pile of letters on your desk.
  Oh, he must have signed them.

Drill 2

Two secretaries are talking in the office.

1 (Example)   I wonder if Tom managed to explain the plan to them.
  Yes, I believe he did get it across.

2 (Example)   I wonder if Eva was given permission to attend the ceremony.
  Yes, I believe she did get off for it.

3 I wonder if Franz recovered from his disappointment.
  Yes, I believe he did get over it.

4 I wonder if the file was returned to Miss Jones.
  Yes, I believe she did get it back.

5 I wonder if Betty was able to take the message down on such a bad line.
  Yes, I believe she did get it down.

6 I wonder if Mr Gräber managed to finish that long report I gave him.
Yes, I believe he did get through it.

7 I wonder if they found some sort of answer to that problem.
Yes, I believe they did get round it.

8 I wonder if Mr Konstanz managed without the overhead projector.
Yes, I believe he did get by without it.

Pronunciation Practice

In this unit we shall study one more intonation pattern for questions. This time we'll look at the intonation of alternative questions. An alternative question is one where there is an *or* in the question form. Like this:

Would you like tea or coffee?

Did you notice the intonation? The speaker's voice goes up on the first alternative, *tea*, and down on the second alternative *coffee*. Listen again.

Would you like tea or coffee?

Now practise the alternative questions that are in your book. Listen and repeat.

Would you like tea or coffee?
Is the meeting on Monday or Tuesday?
Is that spelt with a C or an S?
Shall I show him in or ask him to wait?
Shall I file it or just throw it away?
Is this letter alright or shall I retype it?
Do you want to speak to Mr Gräber or Mr Heine?
Shall I phone him or would you rather I wrote?

Practise that until you can do it really well. When you have done that go on to the limerick for this unit. Listen first.

The appointment is yours, Mrs Moir.
Here's the contract drawn up by our lawyer.
We provide a canteen,
And a good pension scheme:
As you see we're a first-class employer!

Dialogue

Miss Wood, who works in Schweibur's Sales Department, is ringing up Mr Monteiro of Portugal to ask him for information which is missing from his order.

Secretary: Senhor Monteiro's office.

Miss Wood: Good afternoon. Can I speak to Mr Monteiro, please?

Monteiro: Monteiro speaking.

Miss Wood: Good afternoon, Mr Monteiro. This is Miss Wood from Schweibur.

Monteiro: Ah, good afternoon, Miss Wood.

Miss Wood: Thank you very much for your order. We got it this morning.

Monteiro: Oh, good. You can supply us straight from stock, can you?

Miss Wood: Yes, luckily we've got everything you need in stock. There's just one small point, though, to do with the LP desk units. You don't say what kind of wood you want.

Monteiro: Oh, I'm sorry. Teak, please.

Miss Wood: Teak. Well, we'll get those units to you as quick as we can, Mr Monteiro.

Monteiro: Thank you very much. Was there anything else?

Miss Wood: No, that was all, thank you. I just wanted to clear up that point about the kind of wood.

Monteiro: All right. Goodbye, then.

Miss Wood: Goodbye.

Correspondence

In this Key suggestions for an acceptable version are printed in bold type.

Dear Sirs,

We would like to apologize **for the fact that** you had to remind us of your Invoice No 3072/6 due for payment on 19th August. Under normal circumstances such a payment **would have** been made immediately, but the **recent** industrial dispute and **stoppage by** our engineering staff has created quite a few problems for us. **Furthermore**, if some of our own customers had not delayed payment of their debts to us we might well **have been able** to settle at the appropriate time.

We are, however, arranging immediate payment of £5,000 **according to** your instructions. **We are hoping to settle** the balance of the account by 31st September.

We regret that we have been thus obliged to **depart from** our agreement in this respect but trust that you will **bear with us**. We are doing **our utmost** to settle with our suppliers under very difficult circumstances.

Yours faithfully,

Telegrams

We have not remitted the full amount shown on your invoice number 667, because VAT (Value Added Tax) was wrongly charged on Item 4.

All my travellers cheques have been stolen. Could you please arrange for me to draw Fr 1000 at the St Tropez branch of the Credit Lyonnais immediately.

1. VAT NOW CHARGEABLE SUCH GOODS STOP KINDLY REMIT BALANCE AS PER INVOICE

2. ARRANGING FACILITIES FOR FIVE HUNDRED DRAWABLE BOULEVARD GASSIN BRANCH

Language Laboratory Part 2: Tapescript

Drill 3

Mr Braun, the Managing Director, has asked his secretary to find out a number of things for him.

1. (Example) Sales Department, can I help you?
   Good morning. Mr Braun was wondering when the next sales conference is.

2. (Example) Mr Gräber's office.
   Good morning. Mr Braun was wondering whether the visitors have arrived.

3. Head Storeman speaking.
   Good morning. Mr Braun was wondering how many filing cabinets we have in stock.

4. Heine here.
   Good morning. Mr Braun was wondering who is dealing with the Italian order.

5. Purchasing Department.
   Good morning. Mr Braun was wondering whether Mr Fromm is back from Holland yet.

6. Travel Department. Can I help you?
   Good morning. Mr Braun was wondering what time Mr Santos is supposed to be arriving.

7. Mr Gräber's office.
   Good morning. Mr Braun was wondering whether Mr Gräber has got a copy of Mr Karlberger's report.

8. Production here.
   Good morning. Mr Braun was wondering how soon Mr Shermann can give him figures on the TT range.

Drill 4

Schweibur's Chief Accountant, Mr Flügel, sometimes makes unreasonable demands on the typists in his department. His secretary often refuses, politely, to do what her boss asks her.

1. (Example) I wonder if you could finish that report by four o'clock?
   I'm afraid that's out of the question. We couldn't possibly finish it by then.

2. (Example) They're short of a typewriter next door. Do you think you could do without that extra machine?
   I'm afraid that's out of the question. We couldn't possibly do without it.

3. There's going to be a reception for a group of English visitors next week. Can you organize the catering?
   I'm afraid that's out of the question. We couldn't possibly organize it.

4. I wonder if we could fit another desk in this room?
   I'm afraid that's out of the question. We couldn't possibly fit another one in here.

5. We'd have a lot more room if we could get the stationery in the steel cupboard.
   I'm afraid that's out of the question. We couldn't possibly get it in there.

6. We must get these invoices done. Perhaps you'd all be able to come in on Saturday morning.
   I'm afraid that's out of the question. We couldn't possibly come in then.

7. We'll have to go through these petty cash slips before lunch.
   I'm afraid that's out of the question. We couldn't possibly go through them before then.

8. Oh, and one more thing. Make sure you give me your monthly schedules by tomorrow.
   I'm afraid that's out of the question. We couldn't possibly give you them by then.

Active Listening

Passage 1: Listen to this telephone conversation, and then write down the message. You should take notes during the call but do not stop the tape.

Silone: Good morning. Is Mr Schulz there, please?

Secretary: I'm afraid he's out at the moment. Can I help you?

Silone: Well, I wonder if you would be so kind as to take a message for him. My name is Silone, S-I-L-O-N-E. I have written to Mr Schulz asking him to send me a certain document, he will know what I am talking about, but I would like him to send it, not to my usual address which is in the letter, but to the address of our subsidiary c/o 4T Italiana, 76 via Gattamelata, that's G-A- double T- A-M-E-L-A-T-A, 76 via Gattamelata, Turin. I shall be working in Turin for the next two weeks.

Language Laboratory Part 2

Secretary: I see. Right, thank you very much, Mr Silone. I'll ask Mr Schulz to send it on to that address.

Silone: Thank you very much.

Write down the message for Mr Schulz.
Mr Silone rang to ask you to send him the document he has written to you about—he says you will know the one—to:
c/o 4T Italiana
76 via Gattamelata
Turin
as he will be working there for the next two weeks.

Passage 2: Here is another telephone conversation. Listen to it and then write down the message. You should take notes during the call but do not stop the tape.

Morrisson: Good afternoon, I'm ringing from Glasgow and I'd like to speak to Mr Shermann if I could.

Secretary: I'm afraid Mr Shermann isn't in the office at the moment. Would you like to leave a message?

Morrisson: Oh. Well, no, not really. You see, I wanted to put one or two questions to Mr Shermann about your Fonomat Switchboard; there are certain points in the information you sent me that we need urgent clarification on, and I understand Mr Shermann is the person to talk to about this. Look, maybe you could ask him to ring back, today if possible.

Secretary: Yes, he'll be back soon.

Morrisson: Well, my name's Morrisson, two Rs and two Ss, and I'm from Dougall and Dougall, D-O-U-G-A- double L, and the number is Glasgow 3 double 9 462.

Secretary: Alright, Mr Morrisson, I'll ask Mr Shermann to ring you. Thank you very much. Goodbye.

Write down the message for Mr Shermann.
Mr Morrison of Dougall and Dougall, Glasgow, rang to ask you to clarify one or two points about the Fonomat Switchboard. Could you ring him back on Glasgow 399462 today. He says its urgent.

Passage 3: Your boss has recorded the following instruction for you.

I see from our accounts that Martin and Co haven't settled our invoice of 5th September yet. Could you send them a copy of the invoice with a gentle reminder.

What are you to do?
Send Martin and Co a copy of the 5th September invoice, together with a gentle reminder.

Passage 4: Here is another instruction from your boss.

It's been brought to my attention that Cotton Ltd have not settled their account this month. Send them a routine first reminder, with a duplicate of our last invoice.

What are you to do?
Send Cotton Ltd a routine first reminder with a duplicate of our last invoice.

Role Simulation

Situation

The students are asked to imagine that their boss's opposite number from a subsidiary has come to their company for a period. He is sharing an office with their boss and the latter has asked them to explain to the newcomer where everything is kept and what the office procedure is. Students should be encouraged wherever possible to relate what they say to their own office.

Preparation

The students should be forewarned and told to make notes about their own office and the procedures used prior to the class.

Procedure

The teacher should act the role of the visiting executive throughout and should add his own questions to ask the secretary. There are no roles but the secretary should be told to cover as many of the following points as possible.

1. where stationery is kept
2. the procedure for ordering small items
3. petty cash
4. the filing system
5. the procedure for dealing with incoming mail
6. the procedure for dealing with outgoing mail
7. the use of shorthand / audio-typing / typing pool / etc
8. the length of notice needed for typing other than routine mail, etc
9. photocopying and other facilities
10. availability of dictation machine and other equipment
11. the filtering of telephone calls
12. other office routines

Key to 'What is this?'

Page 114: overhead projector
Page 117: tape recorder
Page 120: glue-pot

Unit 11

Unit Summary

Introductory Recording This episode is entitled 'Changing Jobs'. Mary Malone has applied for the job of personal secretary advertised by Alpair, and has been interviewed by Alpair's Personnel Manager, Albert Ehrlich. She hasn't heard from Ehrlich since the interview, and so rings him up while Mr Flügel is temporarily out of the office.

Text The Text is the letter that Ehrlich writes to Mary Malone shortly after her telephone call, offering her the job at Alpair.

Vocabulary Exercise A is a two-part exercise on vocabulary related to job applications and employment.

Structures
1. *Needn't have/Didn't need to* (Exercise B and Drill 1)
   Wasn't able to/Couldn't have
2. Prepositions after verbs and nouns. (Exercise C and Drill 2)

Pronunciation There is an exercise on the shifting of the tonic syllable:
Mr Gräber must endorse all the *cheques*.
Mr Gräber *must* endorse all the cheques.

This is followed by repetition of a limerick practising the vowel sounds [ʊ] as in *cook* and [u] as in *shoe*.

Dialogue The situation is that of telephoning to change the date of an appointment.

Correspondence There is a draft letter to be corrected.

Telegrams There are four telegrams, two to be decoded and two to be encoded.

Gambits Drill 3: Asking for information
Good morning . . . . I wonder if you could help me? I wanted to . . . .

Drill 4: Reassuring people
Don't worry, Mr . . . . Just leave the . . . to us. We'll make sure . . . .

Active Listening There are three passages in this unit. Passage 1 is a telephone message to be written down, and Passages 2 and 3 are recorded instructions from the boss.

Role Simulations

There are ten different Role Simulations in this unit. Each one has a role for use by the students. Each Role Simulation involves meeting a visitor.

The teacher should play the parts of the ten visitors.

Homework

No new gambits are introduced in this unit. The student should draw on gambits she has already met in the course to write the letter.

Introductory Recording

Tapescript

Changing Jobs

Mary Malone has been transferred from Mr Gräber's office to work in the accounts section of Schweibur International. But she has found that she does not care for the type of work she has to do. And her boss, Mr Flügel, seems difficult to please. She has not been happy. So she has applied for another job, with Alpair, the airline.

Flügel: Miss Malone?

Malone: Yes, Mr Flügel.

Flügel: I have to go to the Board meeting now. You will remain in charge of this office. Make a note of any business that requires attention.

Malone: Should I put through any urgent calls?

Flügel: No, that cannot be permitted. Make a note of the name of the caller and tell them I will ring back later if necessary. That is all.

Malone: Yes, Mr Flügel, very well . . . *(Fade)*

Malone: Mr Flügel's office. Can I help you?

Fromm: Fromm. Buying Section. Mr Flügel, please.

Malone: He's just gone to a meeting, I'm afraid, Mr Fromm. Can I take a message? Or ask him to call you back?

Fromm: I think you should have a message from Flügel for me. About some indents, yes?

Malone: Erm, no, I don't think so, Mr Fromm.

Fromm: But he must have told you. I . . .

Malone: He couldn't have, Mr Fromm. I've got no note to that effect at all.

Fromm: Perhaps you forgot to put it down.

Malone: No, Mr Fromm, I did not. Is there anything else now?

Fromm: No, no. I'll call Mr Flügel later, yes? He won't have forgotten, I'm sure.

Introductory Recording

Malone: Goodbye, Mr Fromm . . . *(Fade)*

Receptionist: Alpair.

Malone: Oh, good morning. I wonder. Could I speak to the Personnel Manager. It's about a job application I . . .

Receptionist: Yes. And your name, please?

Malone: Malone. M-A-L-O-N-E. Mary Malone.

Receptionist: And that's Miss Malone?

Malone: Yes, that's right.

Receptionist: Very good, hold the line a moment, please.

Ehrlich: Ehrlich.

Receptionist: A Miss Malone on the phone, Mr Ehrlich.

Ehrlich: Ah, yes, I know. Thank you.

Receptionist: All right. I'll put her through. You're through now.

Ehrlich: Thank you. Hello. Good afternoon, Miss Malone.

Malone: Oh, good afternoon, Mr Ehrlich. I wonder if you can help me? I just wanted to . . .

Ehrlich: I expect it's about your application. Is that right?

Malone: Oh, yes, exactly. I hope you don't mind me ringing about it. Perhaps I shouldn't have. But I was a bit worried . . .

Ehrlich: Oh, no, you needn't have worried. There don't seem to be any problems. But wait a moment. There are one or two things I'd like to ask you. Things we weren't able to finalize when you came for interview.

Malone: Yes, I see. Was it about my references?

Ehrlich: No, not that. In fact, we didn't need to follow them up. I have a contact in Schweibur, you see, where you work, and I've been told that your work is quite up to standard. Rather good, in fact. No. One of the points was salary. Yes. We've got down what you're earning at present. But we couldn't have made a note of what you were hoping for, I mean, what salary you expect, if you were to come to us. Can you, er, . . .

Malone: Well, you see, at the present I would be quite content with the same salary. For the same hours, that is. It's not the pay that I am complaining about it's the . . .

Ehrlich: Yes, well, erm, I think you made that fairly clear when we saw you here. OK. Now, the other question was about notice. You weren't able to be quite definite about that, were you?

Malone: I'm afraid I can't say very much at the moment, either. It's rather difficult, you see . . .

Ehrlich: I think I understand, yes. You don't want to talk to anyone there about it until we had come to some sort of decision on it. Right? Is that the situation?

Malone: Oh, yes, that's exactly it, Mr Ehrlich. Better not to say anything until I know . . .

Ehrlich: Yes, well, I shouldn't worry about it, Miss Malone. Just leave the details to us. We'll make sure everything is arranged properly with your employer.

Malone: Oh, thank you very much. And, er, do you mean . . . . Have I got the job?

Ehrlich: Well, yes, it does begin to seem so, doesn't it? Of course, I couldn't comment on your application officially, not before it's been processed. That wouldn't be correct. But I can tell you there will be a letter coming to you fairly soon. And we're very glad you did apply. We're really in great need of a first-class secretary. And the others we looked at aren't up to much. So . . .

Malone: Oh, that's very good news. Thank you so much. I shall look forward to getting your letter. And thank you again, Mr Ehrlich. Goodbye.

Ehrlich: Yes, goodbye, Miss Malone. We look forward to seeing you here soon.

Comprehension Questions

1 Where was Mr Flügel going?
To the Board meeting.

2 Could Mary have interrupted him if she had wanted to?
No.

3 Who telephoned her soon after Mr Flügel had left?
Mr Fromm.

4 What was Mr Fromm ringing up about?
He thought Mr Flügel would have left a message for him.

5 Who did Mary ring up?
The Personnel Manager of Alpair.

6 Can you remember his name?
Ehrlich.

7 What was Mary ringing him up about?
Her application.

8 Were there any problems about her application?
No, there weren't.

Introductory Recording

9 What were Ehrlich's questions about?
Salary; notice.

10 What did Mary want in the way of salary?
She would be happy with the same salary that she's getting at the moment, for the same hours.

11 Is Mary going to get the job at Alpair?
It's not definite, but all the indications are that she will.

Text: Changing Jobs

Comprehension Questions

The words and phrases in italics are quoted verbatim from the Text.

1 Who is Mr Ehrlich?
Alpair's *Personnel Manager*.

2 Why is he writing to Mary?
To *offer* her *the post of Personal Secretary*.

3 What happened a short while before this letter was written?
Mr Ehrlich interviewed Mary.

4 Has Mary got a job at the moment?
Yes, she has. *(Your present employer.)*

5 Can she leave her job immediately?
No she has to give *one month's notice*.

6 When does Mr Ehrlich want her to start?
On November 1st.

7 What would Mary have to do in her new job?
Act as the Personnel Manager's *Personal Secretary* and organize *the secretarial work of the whole department*.

8 Who would she be responsible to?
The Personnel Manager.

9 How many hours would she work in a week?
Forty.

10 How much would she be paid?
Fr 1,500 per month.

11 When would her salary first be reviewed?
Next *April*.

12 What has Mary got to do now?
Let Alpair *know in writing* as soon as possible whether she wants to *take up the post*.

13 Would you accept the offer? Why / Why not?

Key to the Exercises

Exercise A

2. She wrote asking for further information.
3. She received an application form and details of the job.
4. She filled in the application form and wrote a curriculum vitae.
5. She posted the application.
6. She received an invitation to an interview.
7. She attended the interview.
8. She received a verbal offer of the job.
9. She accepted the offer verbally.
10. She received written confirmation of the offer.
11. She wrote confirming acceptance of the job.
12. She gave notice.
13. She started the job.

2. A vacancy is a job with nobody filling it.
3. A curriculum vitae is a list of qualifications and experience.
4. A reference is a description of someone's character and ability.
5. A short-list is a list of applicants chosen for interview from a larger number.
6. Salary is a monthly payment for work.
7. Notice is an announcement that one is leaving a job.
8. A fringe benefit is something offered in addition to salary.

Exercise B

1. There was such a good response to our advertisement for a secretary that we *didn't need to advertise* more than once. The newspaper cancelled the advert for us after its first appearance.

2. If I had only remembered Miss Berglund we *needn't have spent* so much time interviewing the other candidates.

3. I did my best but there were so many candidates I just *wasn't able to see* them all in the time available. This was an unforseen situation that should not have arisen.

4. I *couldn't have known* about Miss Lejeune when we advertised the vacancy.

5. We had already interviewed her before for a similar post, so fortunately we *didn't need to interview* her again.

6. I remember I *wasn't able to see* her as I was in Geneva at the time.

7. Just a moment. According to my diary I was attending a meeting in Stockholm that afternoon so *I couldn't have been* in Norway.

8. You *needn't have given* me Miss Malone's curriculum vitae, by the way. I already have a copy.

9. The applicants had all been sent details of our pension scheme, so I *didn't need to explain* it. This saved a lot of time.

Key to the Exercises 169

10   And you *needn't have bothered* to explain about sickness benefit. I should have told you I sent all the applicants a copy of our booklet.

11   These dates on the interview form must be wrong. You *couldn't have interviewed* four people at the same time.

12   Unfortunately we *weren't able to offer* the job to Miss Chamberlain, although we would have liked to, as we had already offered it to a Miss Malone.

13   We *didn't need to lay on* a microphone for the guest speakers. The acoustics in the room were extremely good, so we didn't bother.

14   I *wasn't able to convey* our apologies to the auditors, I'm afraid. They had already left.

Exercise C

1   The arrangements for handling visiting VIPs were approved.
2   Agreement was reached on the necessity for a new factory.
3   Mr Shermann presented an analysis of resources as a basis for further discussion of the project.
4   It was decided to seek expert advice on siting the new factory.
5   The possibility of making improvements to existing facilities was discussed.
6   Mr Gräber gave a summary of developments in overseas markets.
7   Mr Braun commented on the sharp rise in expenditure.
8   The explanation for the drastic fall in sales was accepted.
9   Suggestions for a reduction in the labour force were dismissed.
10 Mr Flügel suggested making cuts in the budget for research into new production techniques.
11 A 50 per cent increase in directors' fees was authorized.
12 The Board gave their consent to an increase in the Training Budget.

Language Laboratory Part 1: Tapescript

When there is a lot of work to do, the Personnel Department sometimes hires a temporary typist. This week Miss Schneider is working as a 'temp' in the department, but unfortunately she isn't very good and Miss Craig is rather short with her.

Drill 1

1   (Example)   I've done this report, but Miss Schiller had already done it, I'm afraid.
    Well, you needn't have done it then.

2   (Example)   I think I typed copies of this letter but I can't find them anywhere.
    Well, you couldn't have typed them then.

3   I thought I posted this letter but here it is in the tray.
    Well, you couldn't have posted it then.

4 I made you a cup of coffee but you weren't here to drink it.
Well, you needn't have made it then.

5 I typed these handwritten notes and then Miss Schiller said it wasn't necessary.
Well, you needn't have typed them then.

6 I'm sure I paid for my coffee but everyone says I didn't.
Well, you couldn't have paid for it then.

7 I'm sure I put the letter back in the file, but it isn't here.
Well, you couldn't have put it back then.

8 I asked Mr Schulz for that address, and then found it in the file.
Well, you needn't have asked him then.

Drill 2

Schweibur is rocked by scandal. Unauthorized payments have been made to unknown persons and the auditors have been called. Two of the secretaries are talking about it.

1 (Example) The auditors had a good look round the office.
What did they look at?

2 Mr Braun made a complaint.
What did he complain about?

3 Klaus passed one or two comments.
What did he comment on?

4 The figure for expenditure is a very large amount.
What did it amount to?

5 The auditors had a long talk with Mr Flügel.
What did they talk about?

6 The Board gave their consent.
What did they consent to?

7 They reached a decision yesterday.
What did they decide on?

8 It certainly raised their hopes.
What did they hope for?

Pronunciation

In the last four units we've been practising the intonation of questions. Now let's look at the intonation of statements. Listen to this sentence.

Mr Gräber must endorse all the cheques.

When we make a simple statement of fact, our voices go down on the last important word in the sentence. In that example, *cheques* is the last important word. Listen and repeat the parts of that statement.

cheques
all the cheques
must endorse all the cheques
Mr Gräber must endorse all the cheques.

Now, if we consider that one of the words in that statement is more important than the others, we draw attention to it by making our voice go down on the important word. This downward intonation is very noticeable. Now we're going to say that statement four times, and each time we will make a different word important. Listen carefully and write down which word is important.

1 *Mr Gräber MUST endorse all the cheques.*
2 *Mr Gräber must endorse ALL the cheques.*
3 *Mr GRÄBER must endorse all the cheques.*
4 *Mr Gräber must ENDORSE all the cheques.*

Now here are the correct answers.

In number one the most important word was *must*.
In number two the most important word was *all*.
In number three the most important word was *Gräber*.
In number four the most important word was *endorse*.

Did you get all of these right? If you had any difficulty, go back and listen to the exercise again. Now practise making your voice fall on the important word in the sentence. Look at the sentences in your book.

The most important word is printed in capital letters. Make your voice fall here. Listen and repeat.

1 *The paper clips are on the TOP shelf.*
2 *It ISN'T in the filing cabinet.*
3 *I thought I gave the letter to YOU.*
4 *He SAID he would be in by ten.*
5 *He's arriving on the SECOND of April.*
6 *There isn't much HEADED notepaper left.*

Practise that until you can do it really well. When you've done that, go on the limerick for this unit. Listen to it first.

Said the auditors sadly, 'It looks
As though Schweibur's been hoodwinked by crooks.
We've discovered the ruse,
We have proof and accuse
Mr Flügel of cooking the books!

Dialogue

Mr Heine's secretary, Miss Wood, is ringing up the offices of the BCG company in Paris in order to change the date of an appointment Mr Heine has made to see Mr Legrand.

Secretary: Mr Legrand's office.

Miss Wood: Good morning. This is Mr Heine's secretary at Schweibur speaking.

Secretary: Oh, good morning. What can I do for you?

Miss Wood: I'm afraid something rather urgent has arisen that Mr Heine has to deal with and so he won't be able to keep his appointment with Mr Legrand on Thursday.

Secretary: I see. Would you like to make another appointment?

Miss Wood: Yes, please, if you wouldn't mind. When would be a convenient time for Mr Legrand?

Secretary: Well, he's pretty busy next week, but how about Wednesday morning?

Miss Wood: I'm afraid Mr Heine has appointments for the whole of Wednesday. Other than that he's got a fairly clear week though.

Secretary: The only other time Mr Legrand could possibly manage is Tuesday at two.

Miss Wood: Yes, that'll be convenient for Mr Heine too. We'll make it next Tuesday at two then.

Secretary: I'll let Mr Legrand know.

Miss Wood: And could you please convey our apologies to Mr Legrand, but something completely unforeseen has arisen.

Secretary: It's quite alright. Thank you very much for calling. Goodbye.

Miss Wood: Goodbye, and thank you.

Correspondence

In this Key suggestions for an acceptable version are printed in bold type.

Dear Mr Karlberger,

Thank you very much for your letter of May 16th. I am so sorry **I couldn't meet / wasn't able to meet** you when you called the other day.

I was **most impressed** by your qualifications and **wide** experience **in** our **particular branch** of industry.

Correspondence

Although vacancies for the type of executive you mention do **arise** from time to time, I am afraid **there is no such vacancy** in this company **at present**. I would, however, very much like to meet you and discuss **further** the possibility **of** your joining the company, **should** such a vacancy **arise** in the future.

If you **feel** you would like to talk this **matter** over, could I suggest Thursday, May 24th at 2.00 pm? Could you please **let me know** if this time is not **convenient for you**.

We look forward to **meeting** you.

Yours sincerely,

Telegrams

The arrangements for the conference are all under control. There is no need for you to worry/panic about anything.

We have received Mary Malone's references. Thank you very much.

1 PERSUADE AZIS JOIN US ON UP TO NINE THOUSAND POUNDS ANNUALLY

2 CRISIS YOUR DEPARTMENT STOP RETURN ASAP STOP SORRY

Language Laboratory Part 2: Tapescript

Drill 3

Mr Gräber's secretary has to ring some people up and ask them for information.

1 (Example)   Shermann here.
Good morning Mr Shermann. I wonder if you could help me? I wanted to get hold of Mr Pearson's itinerary.

2 Travel Department, Miss Schmidt.
Good morning Miss Schmidt. I wonder if you could help me? I wanted to find out exactly when Mr Jackson is arriving.

3 Miss Miller speaking.
Good morning Miss Miller. I wonder if you could help me? I wanted to settle the question of Mr Lonsky's accommodation.

4 Fromm.
Good morning Mr Fromm. I wonder if you could help me? I wanted to check the number of XJ storage units we have in stock.

5 Office Services. Marceau here.
Good morning Mr Marceau. I wonder if you could help me? I wanted to ask you if we have a copier which takes large documents.

6 This is Andersson speaking.
Good morning Mr Andersson. I wonder if you could help me? I wanted to confirm that you have received our consignment no 3521.

7 Flügel.
Good morning Mr Flügel. I wonder if you could help me? I wanted to find out where Mr Hoffmann is at the moment.

8 Travel Department, Miss Schmidt speaking.
Good morning Miss Schmidt. I wonder if you could help me? I wanted to enquire about flights from Paris to Rome on Sundays.

Drill 4
A conference on marketing techniques is shortly to be held at Schweibur with guest speakers from ten different countries. Miss Miller has the arrangements well in hand but she has to reassure a number of people who ring her up because they are worried about something to do with the conference.

1 (Example) Mouskouris here. Any news on the publicity for the conference? I'll need some brochures, you know.
Don't worry, Mr Mouskouris. Just leave the publicity to us. We'll make sure the brochures are mailed to you.

2 (Example) This is Bertini speaking. I'm a little anxious about my booking for the conference.
Don't worry, Mr Bertini. Just leave the booking to us. We'll make sure a place is reserved for you.

3 Karlberger here. Isn't there a timetable for the conference yet?
Don't worry, Mr Karlberger. Just leave the timetable to us. We'll make sure the details are sent to you.

4 My name is Gomez. I'm rather worried about the question of accommodation.
Don't worry, Mr Gomez. Just leave the accommodation to us. We'll make sure a room is booked for you.

5 This is Brown here. About the conference. I was wondering, are there any catering arrangements?
Don't worry, Mr Brown. Just leave the catering arrangements to us. We'll make sure meals are laid on for you.

6 Vasseur. I'm rather concerned about transport. We have to get out to you from the airport, you know.
Don't worry, Mr Vasseur. Just leave the transport to us. We'll make sure a car is provided for you.

7 O'Hara here. I'm worried about equipment at the conference. I'll need an overhead projector.
Don't worry, Mr O'Hara. Just leave the equipment to us. We'll make sure an overhead projector is set up for you.

8   This is Deferre speaking. My quiet voice may be a bit of a problem at this conference. I can't speak in a large room without a microphone.
Don't worry, Mr Deferre. Just leave the acoustics to us. We'll make sure a microphone is provided for you.

Active Listening

Passage 1: Listen to this telephone conversation.

Secretary: Mr Heine's office. Good morning.

Kerensky: Could I speak to Mr Heine, please?

Secretary: I'm afraid Mr Heine isn't in yet. Can I take a message?

Kerensky: Yes, please. My name is Kerensky. I'm ringing from the Continental Hotel. I'm supposed to be seeing Mr Heine at ten o'clock this morning, but unfortunately I have a severe headache and I shall have to lie down for a couple of hours. Can you tell Mr Heine I will try to get to his office later this morning. Or in any case I shall ring him at twelve if I'm no better. And please say I'm sorry to have upset Mr Heine's plans like this.

Secretary: Oh, that's quite alright, Mr Kerensky. I'll let Mr Heine know, and I hope you'll feel better later on.

Kerensky: Thank you. Goodbye.

Write down the message for Mr Heine.
Mr Kerensky rang to say he has a severe headache and will not be able to come at ten. He will try to come later, but will ring at twelve if he's no better. He apologizes for any inconvenience he may have caused.

Passage 2: Your boss has recorded the following instruction for you.

There are two job applications in my tray for the new post of product executive. Could you send a standard refusal. Lindburg and, er, Jameson were the names.

What do you have to do?
Send standard letters of refusal to Mr Lindburg and Mr Jameson.

Passage 3: Here is another instruction from your boss.

We had an application from a Mr Byland for the new job. Could you ask him here for an interview, any time from next week on, and sign that in my absence.

What do you have to do?
Write to Mr Byland inviting him for an interview any time after this week. Sign the letter.

Role Simulation

Situation

In this unit the situation varies in each role simulation. The situation is, therefore, outlined in the individual roles.

Preparation

The teacher should study the roles given below and draw up his own roles for the part of the visitor.

Procedure

The teacher should play the part of the visitor throughout. Each student should be given a copy of one of the roles and should act as indicated in it.

Secretary's Roles

1 Your boss has suddenly developed flu and cannot meet Mr Bowes. It is your job to welcome the visitor, and give him a programme for his two-day visit to your company. After explaining the programme and answering any questions he may have, you should offer to take the visitor to his first meeting.

2 The visitor is a Mr Brooks from your company's British subsidiary. He has been seconded to your company for a period of six months. This is his first morning and he is waiting to see your boss. His wife and family have come with him. As this is their first visit here, your boss has asked you to give them as much useful information as you can about shopping, laundry, transport, hairdressers, parking of cars, etc.

3 The visitor is a Professor Mangelbien. He has lost his briefcase containing all his research papers somewhere on the way from West Berlin. The airline has already been contacted and it has been established that the briefcase was not left on the plane. Your job is first to calm Professor Mangelbein down and reassure him that everything will be done to recover his briefcase. You also have to get an exact description of the briefcase and full details of all Professor Mangelbein's movements from the time he landed.

4 A Mr Johnstone has just arrived in your office. He believes he has an appointment with your boss in ten minutes' time. On checking your boss's diary you see that there has been some mistake and that the appointment is down for the following day. You must apologize for the mistake and try to rearrange the appointment on another day. When this proves impossible, you must suggest something of interest for Mr Johnstone to do for the next hour while he is waiting for your boss to return from a meeting.

5 Your boss was rushed off to hospital yesterday for an emergency operation. A visitor by the name of Mr Clayton is expected. You have already arranged for someone else from the Sales Division to see him. You should reassure the visitor that this person is equally competent to deal with his enquiry. You should then give him directions how to get to that person's office, which is some distance away.

6   Jordan and Brown and H E Hewitt are two rival firms of English contractors who are both trying to get a contract from your company. At this very moment Mr Jordan, the Managing Director of Jordan and Brown, is discussing details of the plan with your boss. Very unexpectedly, Mr Hewitt, Managing Director of the rival firm, arrives in your office asking to speak to your boss. He has no appointment. You know the two Englishmen mustn't meet, and you must somehow get Mr Hewitt out of the office but without offending him in any way. You must also avoid answering his questions about the proposed contract and about other firms who might be interested in it.

7   A short while ago your boss rang up to say that his car had broken down and that he would be late for his appointment with Mr Ullabong, an important official from the Ministry of Trade for Takoland, a new African republic. You have been told that this gentleman is easily offended and you know you must do everything you can to keep him in the office until your boss gets back. When he arrives you must apologize for your boss's absence and minimize the delay. You know Mr Ullabong is a great nationalist, in fact he was one of the great freedom fighters who gained independence for his country. Every time he shows impatience or talks of leaving, you must ask him to tell you about his country, new developments there, and his exploits in the war of independence.

8   An important Trade Delegation from Japan is visiting your company. You have been asked to act as a guide for one group of delegates. You are to introduce yourself and then give them a brief history of your company before taking them in to see a film. You should also answer any questions the head of the Delegation asks you about the company.

9   Your company is holding a large conference which is being attended by many of the senior executives of the subsidiaries. A number of these men have brought their secretaries with them to act as interpreters and help in the organization of the conference. You have been asked to share your office with a Miss Bonheim from Switzerland. Your boss has just brought her into the office and you must now make her feel welcome, show her where everything is in the office, tell her about facilities like vending machines or the canteen. When you have done that, find out everything you can about her personal life, without appearing too nosy.

10 The Managing Director of the English subsidiary, Mr Sands, is visiting on business. He has brought his wife with him. They are both in your office now. Mr Sands is going to talk to your boss and you have been asked to entertain the wife until their discussion is over. You must start up a conversation with her.

Key to 'What is this?'

Page 125: adhesive tape ('Sellotape' or 'Scotch' tape) and dispenser
Page 130: ball of string
Page 131: (office) scales

Unit 12

Unit Summary

Introductory Recording	This episode is entitled 'The New Secretary'. Maureen Lynch has replaced Mary Malone as Mr Gräber's secretary. She is not nearly so efficient as Mary and Mr Gräber is complaining about her lack of organization.
Text	The Text is a Memo which Mr Gräber had to write to Maureen about office organization a week later.
Vocabulary	There is one exercise on vocabulary which appears in the Text.

Structures

1. Gerund/Infinitive after certain verbs: (Exercise B and Drills 1 and 2)
   to *avoid do*ing something
   to *fail to* do something

2. Connectors:
   in spite of the fact that / although
   in spite of / despite
   even if
   or else / otherwise

   Exercise D is a short revision exercise.

Pronunciation Practice	There is an exercise on selecting the tonic syllable, and another on the use of a falling-rising intonation pattern. These are followed by repetition of a limerick practising the vowel sounds [eɪ] as in *fate*, and [ɪ] as in *fit*.
Dialogue	The situation is that of dealing with an unexpected caller.
Correspondence	There is a draft letter to be corrected.
Telegrams	There are four telegrams: two to be decoded and two to be encoded.
Gambits	Drill 3: Agreement It looks as if we need another typewriter. *Yes, we certainly* do *need another typewriter.* Polite disagreement: It looks as if we need another typewriter. *Well, I'm not so sure we* do *need another typewriter actually.*
Active Listening	There are three passages in this unit.

1. A recorded instruction
2. A telephone message
3. A dictated letter to be written down in full

Unit Summary

Role Simulation

The students are asked to imagine that the Schweibur Group of companies is very concerned about the high rate of turnover of secretarial staff and the shortage of good replacements for those who leave. Consequently the management have set up a committee from various subsidiaries to discuss the causes of these problems and produce a report of their findings.

Homework

In this unit the students are asked to write up the report on the findings of the Secretaries' Committee in the Role Simulation.

Introductory Recording

Tapescript

The New Secretary

Mary Malone, who was not happy about her transfer from Mr Gräber's office to the Accounts Section, has left Schweibur International and gone to work for an airline. Her friend Maureen Lynch has taken over as secretary to Mr Gräber, but is finding things a little difficult at the moment.

Lynch: Yes, Mr Gräber?

Gräber: Could you come in for a moment, Maureen, please.

Lynch: Oh yes, Mr Gräber.

Gräber: Maureen, where is the Fonomat file?

Lynch: I, I'm not sure Mr Gräber. Do we need to have it today?

Gräber: Yes, we certainly do. Tell me, Maureen, you've been with me how long now?

Lynch: Oh, it's two and a half weeks, I'd say, Mr Gräber.

Gräber: Two and a half weeks. Yes, that's correct. But in spite of that you don't yet seem able to remember to organize things as I have advised you to. You really should be able to put your finger on things I need at a moment's notice. And it shouldn't be necessary for me to remind you quite so often that we must have an efficient office. If we don't, my work will suffer. And that would not be good for me or for you. Do you see?

Lynch: Oh yes, Mr Gräber.

Gräber: Now your friend Mary Malone was a good secretary. She seemed to have no trouble in keeping things in order. Everything at her fingertips in fact. Didn't need to be told what to do. Or to be asked to do routine things. And, er, although she left in rather a hurry, I know, she did spend quite some time putting things straight. Making everything ready for you. Making lists. Have you still got those lists, by the way?

Lynch: Oh yes, Mr Gräber, I have. Somewhere. Probably in my tray . . .

Gräber: Somewhere? That's just it. Look, Maureen, I really must insist on you being more methodical. Or else I may have to start looking for a new secretary. Although I don't want to if I can avoid . . .

Lynch: Well, Mr Gräber, perhaps you should have kept your Mary Malone.

Gräber: Yes, well, erm, that was beyond my control. Internal movements and so on. And irrelevant at this moment. We are trying to persuade you to be more systematic. To use your diary, bring forward things as and when necessary, you see.

Lynch: Oh yes, I do, Mr Gräber. And I will try. I think really I do find the work more difficult than I expected. More to remember and look after. I haven't done much personal secretary work before. But I will try hard to keep up with it.

Gräber: Good, that's fine Maureen. So. I think you should spend some time studying the lists Mary left you. You should do that, shouldn't you?

Lynch: Oh, yes, I should, of course, Mr Gräber.

Gräber: And you see, there are various items that need to be attended to regularly. Making sure that supplies of stationery are sufficient, things like that. Incidentally, do we need anything like that at the moment?

Lynch: Well, I'm not sure we do. But I'll check on it at once.

Gräber: Yes, good. And there's keeping the store cupboards tidy. Having the items all in order. That sort of thing. And the filing system is particularly important, isn't it? We need to attend to that carefully, don't we?

Lynch: Oh yes, we certainly do, Mr Gräber.

Gräber: Yes, and . . . er . . . Oh yes, we should avoid leaving papers for filing too long without attention. Even if there are a lot of other matters to deal with. Nothing worse than looking for a recent document and not . . . er . . . you see?

Lynch: Yes, Mr Gräber.

Gräber: And, of course, papers must be filed correctly. You can consult me if you're in doubt, of course, although there is a list that we prepared. OK?

Lynch: Thank you, Mr Gräber, I will.

Gräber: Fine. Now. Is there anything else we need to talk about just now? Otherwise I must go on with this report.

Lynch: No, I don't think so, Mr Gräber. I'll be outside if you need me.

Gräber: Right. Thank you, Maureen.

Introductory Recording

Lynch: Oh, hello. Can I help you?

Fromm: This is Mr Gräber's office, isn't it?

Lynch: Oh yes it is. I'm his new secretary. Is he expecting you?

Fromm: No, I don't think so. My name's Fromm. Buying Section. And I . . . *(Fade)*

Comprehension Questions

1. Who has taken over Mary Malone's job?
   Her friend Maureen (Lynch).

2. What did Mr Gräber want at the beginning of the recording?
   A file (on the Fonomat).

3. Why is Mr Gräber angry?
   Because Maureen can't find the file.

4. How long has Maureen been with Mr Gräber?
   Two and a half weeks.

5. What comparison can you make between the two secretaries?
   Maureen's not nearly so efficient as Mary.
   Mary was better organized than Maureen.

6. What did Mary do before leaving?
   She got everything ready for Maureen and made lists.

7. Has Maureen studied these lists?
   No, she's not even very sure where they are. She thinks they might be in her in-tray.

8. What does Mr Gräber threaten to do?
   Look for a new secretary.

9. Why does Maureen find the work difficult?
   Because she hasn't done much personal secretary work before.

10. What does Mr Gräber advise Maureen to do?
    To study the lists Mary left.

11. What does Mr Gräber say about the filing?
    He says it should be done regularly and not left for too long.
    He also stresses the importance of filing papers correctly.

Text: The New Secretary

Comprehension Questions

The words and phrases in italics are quoted verbatim from the Text.

1. What did Mr Gräber instruct Maureen to do last week?
   To tighten up on the arrangements for the storage and supply of stationery and equipment.

2   Why is he so annoyed about the cupboards being disorganized?
    Because *he cannot rely on finding even the most essential piece of equipment.*

3   What happened last Friday?
    He *was obliged to spend the best part of half an hour looking for a paper clip.*

4   Where did he eventually find one?
    In a *box hidden under a pile of folders* in Maureen's *in-tray.*

5   What does he expect Maureen to have done by the end of this week?
    To have tidied up the whole office.

6   How much equipment does he want to keep in the steel cupboard in Maureen's office?
    Sufficient to meet immediate needs.

7   Why has a bottle of glue and a ball of string not previously been kept in the office?
    They *have little occasion to use them.*

8   Why does he want each desk to be equipped with things like a pencil sharpener and a ruler, etc?
    So that they will *not have to waste endless time looking for such items of equipment.*

9   Where does he want all stationery stored?
    In the built-in cupboard to the right of the door.

10 What does he remind Maureen to do?
    To label each shelf clearly.

11 Why should this be done?
    So that no one has any trouble finding things.

12 What does he advise Maureen to do?
    To pin up a blank sheet of paper on the inside of the cupboard door.

13 What should she note down on this paper?
    The items she needs to re-order.

14 Should box files be kept flat inside a cupboard?
    No, they *are meant to be stored upright on shelves.*

15 Why must Maureen check the filing cabinet?
    To ensure that all pockets are labelled.

16 What's wrong with the present filing index?
    It *needs updating.*

17 What effect might prompt refiling have on routine typing?
    It might *mean holding* it *up.*

Key to the Exercises

Execise A

1. some Sellotape
2. some copy paper and some carbon paper
3. some string
4. a label
5. drawing pins
6. a punch
7. pockets
8. (a pair of) scissors
9. a ruler
10. some glue
11. some headed notepaper
12. a pencil sharpener
13. an elastic band (a rubber band)
14. either a paper clip or staples
15. a folder or a file

Exercise B

1. You are only obliged *to submit* receipts when *claiming* hotel expenses.
2. You will be (are) invited *to attend* a reception *to meet* Dr Kahn next Monday.
3. I would advise *you to leave* before four to avoid *getting caught* in the rush hour.
4. Try *ringing/to ring* before 10.30. You should have no trouble *getting through* then.
5. Mr Heine insisted *on changing* the filing system. My apologies for not *sending/giving (having sent/given)* you a copy of the new index.
6. They deny *receiving* the goods and now refuse *to settle/pay* the account.
7. *To* prevent *them getting* dirty, I (*would*) suggest *keeping them* in (*using*) a ring binder.
8. I failed *to find* the address in our files so I shall have to put off *writing* till you get back.
9. You can't rely *on getting* them at such short notice unless you (*I*) can persuade *the printers to work/do* overtime.
10. I have been instructed not *to cash* cheques but you are allowed *to borrow* from petty cash.
11. I regret *to tell* you that you can't get out of *going* to the party. They're expecting you *to make/give* a speech.
12. She is quite accustomed to *using* an electric typewriter. You can count on *getting* the report by 3.

Exercise C

1. *In spite of the fact that/Although* the plane was delayed, he managed to attend the meeting.
2. Tell the operator to stop incoming calls *or else/otherwise* we shall be constantly interrupted.
3. *In spite of/Despite* his inexperience he handled the matter competently.

4 I'm afraid they won't get the letter till Tuesday *even if* we post it tonight.
5 *Even if* we work on till six o'clock, we won't get through the agenda.
6 Dr Kahn's visit was a great success *despite/in spite of* the confusion over the arrangements.
7 Leave detailed instructions for the 'temp' *otherwise/or else* she won't know where to start.
8 I can give you some information on prices *although* we don't normally deal with such enquiries.

Exercise D

Betty: *Had you ever heard* of the Malapropezians before they *found* all this oil there?

Maureen: No. They certainly *must have discovered* vast amounts of the stuff, *otherwise/or else* people wouldn't be making all this fuss. Everyone *is talking* about it.

Betty: Just think, if those two Australians *hadn't explored* the islands no one *would ever have known* that all that oil was there.

Maureen: Well, we *needn't have worried* about the world's supply of oil running out as much as we did. The crisis is over now.

Betty: They say *there* has been a terrific economic boom in the islands. All the big industries *are being encouraged/have been encouraged* to move in. I *expect* we *shall be setting up/will set up* a sales company there *fairly/quite/very* soon, *so that* we can take advantage *of* the increase *in* trade.

Maureen: Is it true that Mr Heine is thinking *of going* out there with a view *to* buying some building land?

Betty: Oh, yes. I *have already booked* his ticket. He *is leaving* on the twentieth of next month. He said he *would/will* be away for about a month. He'll have a lot of paper work to do while he's there. *Consequently/Therefore/So* he's insisting *on taking* a secretary with him. I hope he suggests me. I *would* love to go there.

Language Laboratory Part 1: Tapescript

Drill 1

Mr Braun is checking up on a number of points with his secretary.

1 (Example) I hope you got through to our branch in Dublin.
   I had no trouble getting through to them.

2 (Example) I hope Karl had enough sense to take travellers cheques.
   I advised him to take some.

3 I hope you didn't mention the subject.
   I avoided mentioning it.

4   I hope you made sure you kept a copy.
    I insisted on keeping one.

5   I hope you got them to postpone the meeting.
    I persuaded them to postpone it.

6   I hope you have rearranged the stationery cupboards.
    I spent a lot of time rearranging them.

7   I hope you didn't forget to order more carbon.
    I remembered to order some.

8   Have you ordered any more letterheads?
    I didn't need to order any.

Drill 2

Two secretaries in the Travel Department are talking about the impending visit of the Managing Directors of Schweibur's South American subsidiaries.

1   (Example)   They can't stay at the George. Mr Fereira objected.
    Oh, Mr Fereira objected to staying at the George, did he?

2   (Example)   Nobody wants to make a decision. Mr Konstanz has certainly got out of it.
    Oh, Mr Konstanz has got out of making a decision, has he?

3   Well, they must stay at a good hotel. Mr Estefano is accustomed to that.
    Oh, Mr Estefano is accustomed to staying at a good hotel, is he?

4   And somebody ought to draw up a detailed programme, but Mr Schulz is opposed to it.
    Oh, Mr Schulz is opposed to drawing up a detailed programme is he?

5   Mr Braun wants to see them. He's counting on it.
    Oh, Mr Braun is counting on seeing them, is he?

6   And Miss Miller hasn't found a conference room. She's worried about it.
    Oh, Miss Miller is worried about finding a conference room, is she?

7   Mr Konstanz is going to meet them. He's looking forward to it.
    Oh, Mr Konstanz is looking forward to meeting them, is he?

8   And we'll have to work late. Mr Schulz insists on it.
    Oh, Mr Schulz insists on us working late, does he?

Pronunciation Practice

In the last unit we studied the way we make our voice fall on the most important word in the sentence. Which word is most important depends on the meaning we want to convey in the conversation. Look at the sentences in your book. You will hear someone speaking. When they've finished speaking, you'll hear a gong, like this. *(Gong)* You must then complete the conversation using the sentences in your book and making one word more important than the others. You will hear the correct answer after the pause. Here's an example.

Mr Gräber said he had an urgent letter for me to type but I can't find the draft anywhere.
(Gong)
Mr Gräber might have DIC ↘TATED it.
Dictated was the most important word. Now you try.

1   Mr Gräber said he had an urgent letter for me to type but I can't find the draft anywhere.
    (Gong)
    Mr Gräber might have DIC ↘TATED it.
    Dictated was the most important word.

2   Where's Mr Heine? I thought he wasn't leaving till four.
    (Gong)
    He decided to take an ↘ EARLIER flight.
    Earlier was the most important word.

3   I've got a query about these invoices. Should I go to Mr Hoffmann about it?
    (Gong)
    Yes, ↘ HE deals with all the invoices.
    He was the most important word.

4   I thought you had already reminded them about our stationery order. Hasn't it arrived yet?
    (Gong)
    No, we ↘ STILL haven't got it.
    Still was the most important word.

If you found that difficult go back and do that exercise again. Now there's one more intonation pattern which English people use a lot when they speak. It's called a falling-rising intonation. This means that your voice goes down first and then goes up again. English people often use this intonation when then don't want to put their real feelings into words. When we make a statement that we really mean, we use a falling intonation. Like this.

That new secretary is doing very well.
She's very ef ↘ficient.

The second speaker is agreeing with the first speaker. She really thinks the new secretary is good. Now suppose the second speaker didn't really agree with the first speaker. Suppose she wanted to express some reservation or doubt, instead of making her voice go down, her voice would fall first and then rise. Like this.

The new secretary is doing very well.
She's very ef ⩗ficient.

Now what the second speaker really means here is that although the new secretary is efficient there is something else about her that is not so good. By using this falling-rising intonation the second speaker makes it quite clear to her listener that she has some reservation or doubt. Now let's practise that intonation. You will now hear some short conversations. The second speaker's words are printed in your book. Repeat the second speaker's words, paying particular attention to the falling-rising intonation.

1. That new secretary is doing very well.
   She's very ef ︶ficient.

2. I'm sure Mr Schulz must have taken that file.
   It's ︶possible.

3. Is Mary really going to leave?
   That's what she ︶says.

4. Did you enjoy the film?
   It was ↘ quite ↗ good.

5. You can get those letters typed by this afternoon, can't you?
   Well, I'll ︶try.

6. I'm sure Mr Heine can spare ten minutes to see me.
   Well, he's ↘ rather ↗ busy.

Practise that until you can do it really well. And now we come to the last limerick. Listen to it.

Are you bound to a dull occupation?
Do you suffer from male domination?
Lynn, Lucy or Liz,
Miss, Mrs or Ms,
In the Movement you'll find liberation.

Dialogue

A visitor arrives at the office of the Sales Manager of Schweibur. Miss Wood, his secretary, has never met the visitor before, and was not expecting him.

Thorogood: Ah, good morning, is this Heine's office?

Wood: Yes, it is, can I help you?

Thorogood: Well, I was passing through, and thought I'd take the opportunity of having a quick word with him.

Wood: Mr Heine is rather busy at the moment, I'm afraid. Who shall I say would like to see him?

Thorogood: My name's Thorogood.

Wood: I'm sorry, but may I ask which company you come from?

Thorogood: Yes, of course. James and Haltwhistle, Manchester.

Wood: And did you want to see Mr Heine about anything in particular?

Thorogood: Yes, I'm from the Purchasing Department of my company. We're interested in some of your products, particularly in your new ALD range, actually.

Wood: Thank you. If you'd like to give me your coat, Mr Thorogood, I'll see if Mr Heine is free.

Thorogood: Thank you.

Wood: Do sit down, I won't keep you a moment.

Thorogood: Thank you very much. I hope this isn't too inconvenient, is it?

Wood: Not at all. I'm sure Mr Heine will be very pleased to meet you. If you'll excuse me a moment, I'll tell him you're here.

Thorogood: Yes, of course. Thank you.

Correspondence

In this Key suggestions for an acceptable version are printed in bold type.

Dear Sirs,

Thank you for your enquiry **of** 17th November. We **have pleasure in submitting** the following quotation:

1. 20,000 letterheads, printed **in accordance** with the sample you **sent** *(omit)* us some days ago, with amendments **to** the telephone number.   6,000 sw.frcs.

2. 20,000 white envelopes, printed on the flap only as per sample.   5,000 sw.frcs.

3. 15,000 manilla window envelopes, with the address printed in the **bottom left-hand** corner, as per the **attached** sample.   3,000 sw.frcs.

We **note** /**have noted** that these items **are** required **urgently** and **in view of** your **large** /**substantial** order, we are prepared to guarantee delivery **within** seven to ten days.

However we **regret to have to** inform you that **we will have to charge 700 Swiss Francs for delivery. We are no longer able** to deliver free **owing to** the increase **in transport costs. Would you please confirm that this is acceptable to you.**

We have arranged for our representative **to call** on you in the near future. You **can** /**will be able to** take up the question **of hiring** a franking machine with him.

Yours faithfully,

Telegrams

The training course for managers will begin at 7 pm on Sunday the seventeenth of this month when the Chairman of the Group/Company will address the participants.

The only accommodation that is available on the night of the 20th is on the outskirts of the town. I am booking this for you provisionally.

1 CANT TRACE ORDER MENTIONED IN YOUR LETTER OF SIXTEENTH INST STOP HAVE YOU TRIED BASEL FACTORY STOP

2 OCTOBER SALES REPORT SHOWS NIL SALES FOR LM FILING CABINETS STOP CHECK AND CONFIRM STOP

Language Laboratory Part 2: Tapescript

Drill 3

Mr Konstanz, Schweibur's Training Manager, is discussing the question of the arrangements for typing with his secretary, Miss Miller.

1 (Example) It looks as if we need another typewriter.
Yes, we certainly do *need another typewriter.*

2 (Example) Don't you think we should scrap the manual machine?
Yes, we certainly should *scrap the manual machine.*

3 I suppose we'll have to get a temp in.
Yes, we certainly will *have to get a temp in.*

4 The new girl has done well anyway.
Yes, she certainly has *done well.*

5 The volume of typing is going to fall.
Yes, it certainly is *going to fall.*

But sometimes Miss Miller doesn't agree with what her boss says.

1 (Example) It looks as if we need another typewriter.
Well, I'm not so sure we do *need another typewriter actually.*

2 (Example) Don't you think we should scrap the manual machine?
Well, I'm not so sure we should *scrap the manual machine actually.*

3 I suppose we'll have to get a temp in.
Well, I'm not so sure we will *have to get a temp in actually.*

4 The new girl has done well anyway.
Well, I'm not so sure she has *done well actually.*

5 The volume of typing is going to fall.
Well, I'm not so sure it is *going to fall actually.*

Now you must take the part of the secretary again and this time you must agree with some of the things Mr Konstanz says and disagree with others. The notes will tell you how to answer.

1. It looks as if we need another typewriter.
   Yes, we certainly do *need another typewriter*.

2. Don't you think we should scrap the manual machine?
   Well, I'm not so sure we should *scrap the manual machine actually*.

3. I suppose we'll have to get a temp in.
   Yes, we certainly will *have to get a temp in*.

4. The new girl has done well anyway.
   Yes, she certainly has *done well*.

5. The volume of typing is going to fall.
   Well, I'm not so sure it is *going to fall actually*.

6. I think we should take on another full-time typist, don't you?
   Well, I'm not so sure we should *take on another full-time typist actually*.

7. It's difficult to get new staff, of course.
   Yes, it certainly is *difficult to get new staff*.

8. At any rate Miss Walter ought to spend less time on the filing.
   Yes, she certainly ought *to spend less time on the filing*.

9. Mrs Bonheim could deal with the filing, couldn't she?
   Well, I'm not so sure she could *deal with the filing actually*.

10. Miss Lindburg managed it competently enough.
    Well, I'm not so sure she did *manage it competently enough actually*.

Active Listening

Passage 1: Your boss has recorded the following instruction for you.

Something has gone wrong with my little photocopier; it doesn't seem to be working at all. Could you give Office Equipment a ring and try to get them to see to it before I get back from Italy.

What are you to do?
Telephone Office Equipment to get them to fix the boss's photocopier before he gets back from Italy.

Passage 2: Listen to the following telephone call, and then write down the message. You may take notes during the call, but do not stop the tape.

Ironmonger: Good morning. Could I speak to Mr Heine, please?

Wood: I'm afraid he's out at lunch just at the moment. Can I take a message?

Ironmonger: Well, could you ask him to ring me back as soon as possible please. The name's Ironmonger, I-R-O-N-M-O-N-G-E-R, from Ackroyd and Illingworth and the number's Leeds 73926. Have you got that?

Wood: I'm sorry, I didn't quite catch the telephone number.

Ironmonger: Leeds 73926.

Wood: And can you give me some indication of what you wanted to talk to Mr Heine about, please?

Ironmonger: Yes, it's about a J20 copying machine you supplied to us.

Wood: Right, thank you very much, Mr Ironmonger. I'll pass that on to Mr Heine.

Ironmonger: Thank you and goodbye.

What is the message Miss Wood is to give Mr Heine?
Mr Ironmonger from Ackroyd and Illingworth rang. He wants you to ring him back as soon as possible (Leeds 73926). It's about the J20 copying machine.

Passage 3: Before going off on a sales trip, Mr Heine dictated the following draft of a letter.

Letter to James Hetherington, O'Neil & Co, Dublin. Er, ah, hm, yes: draft a letter making the following points. Thank him for his letter, asking us for an extra discount of 2 per cent over our usual. Tell him that although we welcome his order, appreciate it and all that, our prices are already cut to the minimum. Tell him that if he were to raise his order to, shall we say, hm, by er, 100 of each of the parts, no, make that 150, parts that he orders, we should be pleased to allow him the discount he asks. Finish off by saying that we, er, await his confirmation before we deal with his order, or some such suitable phrase. Oh, just before that last paragraph add that we are sure he will need the extra parts in the foreseeable future anyway. Tone of the letter to be friendly, polite, but make it firm.

Now draft this letter according to Mr Heine's instructions and show it to your teacher.

Role Simulation

Situation

The students are asked to imagine that the Schweibur Group of companies is very concerned about the high rate of turnover of secretarial staff and the shortage of good replacements for those who leave. Many secretaries leave the company after only a year or eighteen months' service. The management have set up a committee of secretaries from the various subsidiaries and have invited them to Headquarters for a two-day seminar.

	The object of this is to discuss the causes of these problems and to produce a report of their findings. They have been asked to make recommendations to management as to what measures can be taken in order to make the post of secretary and typist more attractive.
Procedure	In the final unit the Role Simulation breaks the pattern of the preceding units. Instead of individual role simulations, the whole class takes part. They are the committee set up by management. They should elect a chairperson and draw up an agenda before starting, and one secretary should be detailed to keep the minutes of the discussion.
Note	The teacher may prefer to ask the students to carry out this Role Simulation with reference to their own company or organization, rather than Schweibur.

Key to 'What is this?'

Page 136: coat-hanger
Page 139: wallet
Page 141: hold-all
Page 142: handbag